Focus on Grammar

WORKBOOK

An
INTERMEDIATE
Course for
Reference
and Practice

Marjorie Fuchs

Addison-Wesley Publishing Company
Reading, Massachusetts • Menlo Park, California
New York • Don Mills, Ontario • Wokingham, England
Amsterdam • Bonn • Sydney • Singapore • Tokyo
Madrid • San Juan • Paris • Seoul, Korea • Milan
Mexico City • Taipei, Taiwan

Focus on Grammar: An Intermediate Course for
Reference and Practice Workbook

Editorial Director: Joanne Dresner
Development Editor: Joan Saslow
Production Editorial: Helen B. Ambrosio, Lisa A. Hutchins
Text Design: Six West Design
Cover Design: A Good Thing, Inc.

ISBN 0-201-65687-6

1 2 3 4 5 6 7 8 9 10-VG-9897969594

Contents

About the Author

Marjorie Fuchs taught ESL for eight years at New York City Technical College and LaGuardia Community College of the City University of New York and EFL at the Sprach Studio Lingua Nova in Munich, Germany. She has authored or co-authored many widely used ESL textbooks, notably *On Your Way, Crossroads, Top Twenty ESL Word Games, Around the World: Pictures for Practice, Families: Ten Card Games for Language Learners*, and the *Workbooks* to the *Longman Dictionary of American English, The Longman Photo Dictionary*, and the *Vistas* series.

1. Spelling

Add **-ing** to these verbs to form the present participle. Make spelling changes where necessary.

1. start ___*starting*___   11. visit _____

2. get _____   12. forget _____

3. try _____   13. hurry _____

4. plan _____   14. begin _____

5. have _____   15. decide _____

6. do _____   16. answer _____

7. match _____   17. happen _____

8. grab _____   18. determine _____

9. give _____   19. entertain _____

10. say _____   20. continue _____

Present Progressive

2. Affirmative Statements

Read and complete these postcards with the present progressive form of the verbs in the boxes.

| blow | build | fly | shine | ~~sit~~ |

1

Dear Margaret,

Hi! I'___*m sitting*___ on the beach under a big, bright umbrella. The
1.

weather is beautiful. The sun _____, and there isn't a cloud
2.

in the sky. A soft breeze _____. Some tropical birds (I don't
3.

know what kind) _____ above. Children _____
4.   **5.**

sand castles. This is the place to be!

Wish you were here,
Alice

(Continued on next page.)

1

| get | stand | start | take | travel |

2

Dear Rick,

Susan and I _____ through England. Right now I
1.

_____ in front of Buckingham Palace. It's a cloudy
2.

day. The sky _____ darker by the minute. Molly
3.

_____ pictures. Oh, no! It _____ to rain.
4.   5.

See you in a few weeks!

Mark

| help | improve | live | study | try |

3

Dear Jane,

Here I am in Paris! I _____ French and
1.

_____ with a French family—the Michauds. My
2.

French _____ a lot because I have to speak it "at home."
3.

The Michauds are great. They _____ me find a job.
4.

I _____ to save enough money to travel in August. Why
5.

don't you come and visit me? It's great here!

Elise

3. Yes/No Questions and Short Answers

Look at the postcards in Exercise 2. Ask questions and give short answers.

POSTCARD 1

1. Alice/swim?

   A: *Is Alice swimming?*

   B: *No, she isn't.*

2. it/rain?

   A: _____

   B: _____

3. the children/build sand castles?

   A: _____

   B: _____

POSTCARD 2

4. Susan and Rick/travel in Spain?

   A: _____

   B: _____

5. the sun/shine?

   A: _____

   B: _____

6. Molly/take pictures?

   A: _____

   B: _____

POSTCARD 3

7. Elise/practice her French?

   A: _____

   B: _____

8. she/enjoy her summer?

   A: _____

   B: _____

(Continued on next page.)

9. she/work?

A:_____

B:_____

4. Affirmative and Negative Statements

Look at the picture and read the news report. Chuck Andrews, the reporter, has five of the facts wrong. Find and correct the mistakes.

GENERAL HOSPITAL

Chuck: I'm standing in front of Memorial Hospital. As you can see, the sun is shining. Smoke is coming from the second-floor windows. The fire fighters are trying to put out the fire. One fire fighter is carrying a man down the ladder. Right now, three more fire engines are arriving at the scene. We'll have more on this breaking story later. This is Chuck Andrews reporting live for Channel 3.

1. *He isn't standing in front of Memorial Hospital.*

   He's standing in front of General Hospital.

2. _____

   _____

3. _____

   _____

4. _____

   _____

5. _____

   _____

5. Wh– Questions

Complete the questions. Use the words in parentheses ( ).

1. **A:** What ___*are you doing*_____?

   (you/do)

   B: I'm watching the news.

2. **A:** Which channel _____?

   (you/watch)

   B: Channel 3.

3. **A:** Who _____ the news?

   (report)

   B: Chuck Andrews.

4. **A:** What _____?

   (happen)

   B: There's a fire at General Hospital.

(Continued on next page.)

5. **A:** What _____?
(fire fighters/do)

   B: They're trying to put out the flames, and they're getting the victims out of the building.

6. **A:** Where _____ them?
(they/take)

   B: They're taking them to another hospital.

7. **A:** How _____?
(the victims/do)

   B: They're doing OK. They got out just in time.

2

Simple Present Tense

▼

1. Spelling

Add -s or -es to form the third-person-singular form of these verbs. Make spelling changes where necessary.

1. want	*wants*	11. call	
2. study		12. swim	
3. work		13. happen	
4. hope		14. do	
5. live		15. say	
6. reach		16. have	
7. rush		17. try	
8. know		18. buy	
9. marry		19. go	
10. pay		20. pass	

2. Affirmative Statements

Mario and Silvia are students. Look at what they do every day. Write sentences about their activities.

MARIO		SILVIA	
A.M.		A.M.	
7:30	get up	7:30	get up
8:00	watch TV	8:00	listen to the radio
8:30	go to school	8:30	go to school
P.M.		P.M.	
12:00	have lunch	12:00	have lunch
3:00	study at the library	3:00	play basketball
4:00	go home	4:00	visit her grandmother
5:00	do homework	5:00	do homework
6:00	have dinner	6:00	practice the guitar
7:00	play computer games	7:00	make dinner
8:00	read the newspaper	8:00	wash the dishes

(Continued on next page.)

1. At 7:30 A.M., _*Mario and Silvia get up.*_

2. At 8:00 A.M., _*Mario watches TV. Silvia listens to the radio.*_

3. At 8:30 A.M., _____

4. At 12:00 P.M., _____

5. At 3:00 P.M., _____

6. At 4:00 P.M., _____

7. At 5:00 P.M., _____

8. At 6:00 P.M., _____

9. At 7:00 P.M., _____

10. At 8:00 P.M., _____

3. Yes/No Questions and Short Answers

Look at the schedules in Exercise 2. Ask and answer the questions.

1. Mario and Silvia/go to school?

   A: _*Do Mario and Silvia go to school?*_

   B: _*Yes, they do.*_

2. Mario and Silvia/get up at the same time?

   A: _____

   B: _____

3. Silvia/watch TV in the morning?

   A: _____

   B: _____

4. she/listen to the radio?

   A: _____

   B: _____

5. Mario/study at the library?

   A: _____

   B: _____

6. he/do his homework at school?

   A: _____

   B: _____

7. Silvia/play basketball?

   A: _____

   B: _____

8. Mario/play computer games before dinner?

   A: _____

   B: _____

9. Mario and Silvia/eat dinner together?

   A: _____

   B: _____

10. Silvia/wash the dishes after dinner?

   A: _____

   B: _____

4. Adverbs of Frequency

Put these words in the correct order to form statements.

1. Mario/the newspaper/reads/always

   Mario always reads the newspaper.

2. on time/usually/Silvia/is

   _____

3. never/school/Silvia and Mario/miss

   _____

4. do/their homework/Silvia and Mario/always

   _____

5. is/Mario/tired/often

   _____

(Continued on next page.)

6. usually/eat/the students/in school/lunch

_____

7. hungry/they/are/always

_____

8. gets up/rarely/Silvia/late

_____

5. Wh– Questions and Answers

Ray Mano is a famous TV talk show host. Look at his schedule and complete the interview with Mano.

★ SCHEDULE ★

THE NIGHT SHOW

P.M.

2:30	arrive at the studio
5:00–5:30	talk to the TV audience
5:30–6:30	tape The Night Show
7:00	arrive home
8:00–9:00	work in the garage
10:00–12:00	write jokes

A.M.

12:00–4:00	meet with other writers
4:00–8:00	sleep

1. What time/you/arrive at the studio?

Interviewer: *What time do you arrive at the studio?*

Ray: *At 2:30 P.M.*

2. What/you/do before the show?

Interviewer: _____

Ray: _____

3. How long/you/talk to the audience?

Interviewer: _____

Ray: _____

4. When/you/tape the show?

Interviewer: _____

Ray: _____

5. How long/the show/last?

Interviewer: _____

Ray: _____

6. Where/you/go after the show?

Interviewer: _____

Ray: _____

7. What/you/do at home?

Interviewer: _____

Ray: _____

8. When/you/write new jokes?

Interviewer: _____

Ray: _____

9. How long/you/work with other writers?

Interviewer: _____

Ray: _____

10. How many hours/you/sleep?

Interviewer: _____

Ray: _____

6. Affirmative and Negative Statements

The interviewer in Exercise 5 wrote a short article about Ray Mano, but she got five of the facts wrong. Find and correct the mistakes.

Talk-show host and comedian Ray Mano works unusual hours. He gets up at 8:00 and goes directly to his studio. Mano loves his studio audience and always talks to them after each show.

The Night Show lasts a half-hour. After the taping, Mano goes home and works in his garage on the cars and motorcycles that he collects. He then writes screenplays for two hours. At midnight, Mano and a group of writers meet in his kitchen for three hours. There they plan the next show. At 4:00 A.M., Mano calls it a day and goes to bed for a whole four hours. The life of a comedian is no laughing matter!

1. *He doesn't go directly to his studio.*

   He goes to the studio in the afternoon.

2. _____

   _____

3. _____

   _____

4. _____

   _____

5. _____

   _____

1. Simple Present Tense or Present Progressive

Complete the chart about a businesswoman, Laura DeSoto. What does she usually do? What is she doing today?

USUALLY	TODAY
1. Laura DeSoto gets up at 7:00.	_She is getting up_ at 8:00.
2. _She takes_ the bus to work.	She is taking the train to work.
3. _____ a magazine.	She is reading the paper.
4. She drinks a cup of coffee.	_____ a cup of tea.
5. _____ pants.	She is wearing a dress.
6. _____ lunch in the office.	She is eating lunch in a coffee shop.
7. She wants a small lunch.	_____ a big lunch.
8. _____ English.	She is speaking Spanish.
9. She seems relaxed.	_____ nervous.
10. She goes home late.	_____ home early.

2. Simple Present Tense or Present Progressive

Complete the sentences about a businessman, Tony Martin. Use the correct form of the verbs in parentheses ( ).

1. It's 8:00 A.M. Tony Martin _is driving_ to work. (drive)
2. He _____ to work every day. (drive)
3. The trip usually _____ 45 minutes. (take)
4. Today it _____ longer. (take)
5. Workers _____ the highway this morning. (repair)
6. Because of the construction, Tony _____ Parson Road. (use)
7. Normally, he _____ Route 93. (take)
8. Traffic always _____ faster on Route 93. (move)
9. Today, the weather _____ the traffic, too. (slow down)
10. It _____ hard, and the roads are slippery. (rain)

(Continued on next page.)

13

11. Tony is a careful driver. He always _____ slowly when the roads are wet.
(drive)

12. The radio is on, and Tony _____ the traffic report.
(listen to)

13. He always _____ the radio on his way to work.
(listen to)

14. The announcer _____ an accident on Parson Road.
(describe)

15. Tony _____ to be late for work, but there is nothing he can do.
(not want)

16. Traffic _____ even more slowly because of the accident.
(move)

17. Tony _____ to drive even when the traffic is bad.
(like)

18. He always _____ relaxed when he is behind the wheel.
(feel)

19. He _____ he can't do anything about the traffic conditions.
(know)

20. Tony _____ what psychologists call a Type B personality.
(have)

3. Correct the Mistakes

Read this student's letter. There are eight mistakes in the use of the simple present tense and present progressive.

> Dear Pat,
>
> Hi. How are you? I ~~write~~ 'm writing you this letter on the bus.
> Guess what? I am having a job as a clerk in the mail
> room of a small company. The pay isn't good, but I'm
> liking the people there. They're all friendly, and we are
> speaking English all the time. I'm also taking an
> English class at night at the Adult Center. The class is
> meeting three times a week. It just started last week, so
> I'm not knowing many of the other students yet. They
> seem nice, though.
>
> What do you do these days? Do you still look for
> a new job?
>
> Please write when you can. I always like to hear
> from you.
>
> Yours,
>
> Bill

1. Affirmative and Negative Imperatives

Complete the chart. Use the words in the box.

backward	in	~~left~~	off	tight
down	late	low	shut	up

AFFIRMATIVE	**NEGATIVE**
1. Bend your *right* leg.	*Don't bend your left leg.*
2. _____	Don't look *up*.
3. Lean *forward*.	_____
4. Breathe *out*.	_____
5. _____	Don't keep your eyes *open*.
6. Wear *loose* clothes.	_____
7. Turn the lights *on*.	_____
8. _____	Don't turn the music *down*.
9. _____	Don't put the air conditioner on *high*.
10. Come *early*.	_____

2. Affirmative and Negative Imperatives

Ada, a student, is asking her friends for directions to Jim's Gym. Look at the map and complete the conversation. Use the words in the box.

~~ask~~	continue	go	make	ride	~~take~~	walk
be	cross	have	pass	stop	turn	work

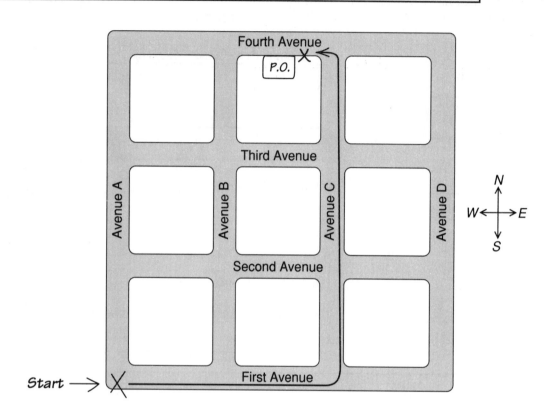

Ada: I'm going to take an exercise class at Jim's Gym. Do you know how to get there?

Bob: Jim's Gym? _____*Ask*_____ Chen. He's taking a class there.
                              1.

Ada: I didn't know that. Which bus do you take to the gym, Chen?

Chen: Oh, _____*don't take*_____ the bus! It's not far from here. _____ or
                         2.   3.
_____ your bike. It's good exercise!
            4.

Ada: I'll walk. How do I get there?

Chen: _____ two blocks east on First Avenue.
                  5.

Ada: East? You mean turn left?

Chen: No. _____ left. Go right when you leave the building. OK? Then
             6.

_____ a left turn when you get to Avenue C. _____ on Avenue C,
    7.   8.

but _____ when you reach Fourth Avenue. _____ Fourth
      9.   10.

Avenue. It's another left at Fourth. But _____ careful. Jim's Gym is small and it's
                              11.

easy to miss. _____ the post office. The gym is just a few buildings before it.
          12.

Ada: Thanks.

Chen: Sure. _____ fun! _____ too hard!
          13.   14.

5

Simple Past Tense

▼

PART II: PAST

Spelling: Regular and Irregular Simple Past Tense Forms

Complete the chart.

BASE FORM	SIMPLE PAST	BASE FORM	SIMPLE PAST
1. answer	*answered*	13. live	
2. buy	*bought*	14. meet	
3. catch		15. need	
4. do		16. open	
5. look		17. put	
6. find		18. read	
7. give		19. say	
8. hurry		20. think	
9. see		21. understand	
10. die		22. vote	
11. kiss		23. win	
12. come		24. feel	

25. The past of *be* is _____ or _____.

2. Affirmative and Negative Statements with the Past Tense of Be

Look at the chart of famous writers of the past. Complete the sentences with **was, wasn't, were,** *and* **weren't.**

Isaac Babel	1894–1941	Russia	short-story writer, playwright*
James Baldwin	1924–1987	United States	author, playwright
Honoré de Balzac	1799–1850	France	novelist
Simone de Beauvoir	1908–1966	France	novelist, essayist**
Giovanni Boccaccio	1313–1375	Italy	poet, storyteller
Karel Čapek	1890–1939	Czechoslovakia	novelist, essayist
Agatha Christie	1891–1976	England	mystery writer
Lorraine Hansberry	1930–1965	United States	playwright
Pablo Neruda	1904–1973	Chile	poet

 *A *playwright* is a person who writes plays.
**An *essayist* is a person who writes essays.

1. Simone de Beauvoir _____*wasn't*_____ a French poet. She _____*was*_____ a French novelist.

2. Giovanni Boccaccio _____ born in 1313.

3. James Baldwin and Lorraine Hansberry _____ American poets. They _____ playwrights.

4. Karel Čapek _____ a poet.

5. Pablo Neruda _____ from Chile.

6. Honoré de Balzac _____ a playwright. He _____ a novelist.

7. Agatha Christie _____ American. She _____ English.

8. Isaac Babel _____ Russian. He _____ French.

9. Simone de Beauvoir and Honoré de Balzac _____ both French.

10. Pablo Neruda and Simone de Beauvoir _____ both born in the early 1900s.

3. Questions and Answers with the Past Tense of Be

Ask and answer questions about the people in Exercise 2. Use **was** *and* **wasn't**.

1. James Baldwin/a playwright?

   A: *Was James Baldwin a playwright?* _____

   B: *Yes, he was.* _____

2. Where/Simone de Beauvoir from?

   A: _____

   B: _____

3. What nationality/Pablo Neruda?

   A: _____

   B: _____

4. Who/Boccaccio?

   A: _____

   B: _____

5. Agatha Christie/French?

   A: _____

   B: _____

(Continued on next page.)

6. What nationality/Lorraine Hansberry?

A: _____

B: _____

7. Honoré de Balzac/a poet?

A: _____

B: _____

8. When/Karel Čapek/born?

A: _____

B: _____

9. Who/Isaac Babel?

A: _____

B: _____

4. Affirmative Statements

Complete these short biographies. Use the simple-past-tense form of the verbs in the boxes.

~~be~~	die	include	spend	translate	write

1. **Lin Yutang** (1895–1976) _____*was*_____ a Chinese-American writer. He _____
   1.   2.
most of his life in the United States. Dr. Lin _____ a lot about his native China. His
                                                3.
books _____ several novels. He also _____ other people's works. Lin
         4.   5.
_____ at the age of 81.
   6.

be	begin	call	have	live	paint

2. **Anna Mary Robertson Moses** (1860–1961) _____ an American painter. She
                                                  1.
_____ on a farm in New York State. Because she _____ painting in her
   2.   3.
seventies, people _____ her Grandma Moses. She never _____ any
                     4.   5.
formal art training. Moses _____ simple, colorful scenes of farm life.
                              6.

be	build	fly	last	take place	watch

3. **Orville Wright** (1871–1948) and **Wilbur Wright** (1867–1912) _____ American airplane inventors. The two brothers _____ their first planes in their bicycle shop in Ohio.
On December 17, 1903, Orville _____ their plane, *Flyer 1*, a distance of 120 feet. Wilbur,
four men, and a boy _____ from the ground. This first controlled, power-driven flight
_____ near Kitty Hawk, North Carolina. It _____ only about 12 seconds.

1.   2.   3.   4.   5.   6.

5. Questions and Answers

Ask and answer questions about the people in Exercise 4.

BIOGRAPHY 1

1. When/Lin Yutang/live?

   A: *When did Lin Yutang live?*

   B: *He lived from 1895 to 1976.*

2. What/he/do?

   A: _____

   B: _____

3. he/write poetry?

   A: _____

   B: _____

4. Where/he/spend most of his life?

   A: _____

   B: _____

BIOGRAPHY 2

5. What/people/call Anna Mary Robertson Moses?

   A: _____

   B: _____

(Continued on next page.)

6. What/she/do?

   A: _____

   B: _____

7. When/she/begin painting?

   A: _____

   B: _____

8. she/have formal art training?

   A: _____

   B: _____

BIOGRAPHY 3

9. Where/the Wright brothers/build their first planes?

   A: _____

   B: _____

10. both brothers/fly the *Flyer 1*?

    A: _____

    B: _____

11. Where/first controlled flight/take place?

    A: _____

    B: _____

12. How long/the flight/last?

    A: _____

    B: _____

6. Negative Statements

There were a lot of similarities between the Wright brothers. But there were also differences. Complete the chart about the differences between Orville and Wilbur.

ORVILLE	WILBUR
1. Orville talked a lot	*Wilbur didn't talk a lot.*
2. *Orville didn't spend a lot of time alone.*	Wilbur spent a lot of time alone.
3. _____	Wilbur had serious health problems.
4. Orville grew a moustache.	_____
5. _____	Wilbur lost most of his hair.
6. Orville took courses in Latin.	_____
7. Orville liked to play jokes.	_____
8. Orville dressed very fashionably.	_____
9. Orville played the guitar.	_____
10. _____	Wilbur built the first glider.
11. _____	Wilbur made the first attempts to fly.
12. _____	Wilbur chose the location of Kitty Hawk.
13. Orville had a lot of patience.	_____
14. Orville lived a long life.	_____

6

Used to

▼

1. Affirmative Statements

Life in the United States isn't the way it used to be. Complete the chart.

IN THE PAST	NOW
1. _People used to ride_ horses.	People ride in cars.
2. _____ by candlelight.	People read by electric light.
3. _____ over open fires.	People cook in microwave ovens.
4. _____ in propeller airplanes.	People fly in jet planes.
5. _____ large families.	People have small families.
6. _____ all of their clothes by hand.	People wash most of their clothes in washing machines.
7. _____ manual typewriters.	People use word processors and computers.
8. _____ twenty-five days to get a message from New York to San Francisco.	It takes just a few seconds.

2. Affirmative and Negative Statements

Complete the sentences about the assistant manager of a California bank, Yoko Shimizu. Use **used to** *or* **didn't use to** *and the verbs in parentheses ( ).*

1. Yoko _____ _used to be_ _____ a full-time student. Now she has a job at a bank.
    (be)

2. She _____ with a computer. Now she uses one every day.
    (work)

3. She _____ a car. Now she owns a 1993 Toyota Corolla.
    (have)

4. Yoko _____ the bus to work. Now she drives.
    (take)

5. The bus _____ crowded. These days it's difficult to find a seat.
    (be)

6. Yoko _____ New York. Then she moved to Los Angeles.
    (live)
    (like)

7. She _____ Los Angeles. Now she thinks it's a nice city.

8. She _____ a lot of people in Los Angeles. Now she has a lot of friends there.
   (know)

9. She _____ to New York several times a year. These days she doesn't go
   (return)
   there very often.

10. She _____ a lot of letters. Now she makes a lot of phone calls instead.
    (write)

3. Questions and Answers

*Look at these two ID cards. Ask and answer questions about Sara Rogers, a new employee at City Savings Bank. Use **used to** and the cues in parentheses ( ).*

THEN   NOW

CITY COLLEGE

[ ] Ms.
[ ] Mr.
[x] Mrs.
[ ] Miss   Sara Rogers-Gordon
           Name
Address: 20 E. 15 St.
          New York, NY 10003
STUDENT ID

CITY SAVINGS BANK *Employee ID*

[x] Ms.
[ ] Mr.
[ ] Mrs.
[ ] Miss   *Sara Rogers*
           Name
Address: *5432 Orange St.*
          Los Angeles, CA 90048 $

1. (live in California?)

   A: *Did she use to live in California?*

   B: *No, she didn't.*

2. Sara recently moved to Los Angeles. (Where/live?)

   A: _____

   B: _____

3. This is her first job. (What/do?)

   A: _____

   B: _____

4. Sara looks very different from before. She has short hair and wears glasses. (have long hair?)

   A: _____

   B: _____

(Continued on next page.)

5. (wear glasses?)

A: _____

B: _____

6. Sara's last name is different from before. (be married?)

A: _____

B: _____

1. Affirmative and Negative Statements with the Past Progressive

Frank Cotter is a financial manager. Look at his schedule and complete the sentences.

10
Wednesday

9:00–10:00	meet with Ms. Jacobs
10:00–11:00	write financial reports
11:00–12:00	answer correspondence
12:00–1:00	eat lunch with Mr. Webb at Sol's Cafe
1:00–3:00	attend lecture at City University
3:00–4:00	discuss budget with Allen
4:00–5:00	return phone calls

1. At 9:30 Mr. Cotter _____ *was meeting with* _____ Ms. Jacobs.

2. At 9:30 he _____ financial reports.

3. At 11:30 he _____ correspondence.

4. At 12:30 he and Mr. Webb _____ lunch.

5. They_____ at Frank's Diner.

6. At 2:00 he _____ a lecture.

7. At 3:30 he and Allen _____ financial reports.

8. They_____ the budget.

9. At 4:30 he_____ correspondence.

10. He _____ phone calls.

2. Questions and Answers with the Past Progressive

Look at the schedule in Exercise 1. Ask questions and give short answers.

1. Mr. Cotter/meet/with Mr. Webb at 9:30?

   A: *Was Mr. Cotter meeting with Mr. Webb at 9:30?*

   B: *No, he wasn't.*

2. What/he/do at 9:30?

   A: _____

   B: _____

3. Mr. Cotter/write police reports at 10:30?

   A: _____

   B: _____

4. What kind of reports/he/write?

   A: _____

   B: _____

5. What/he/do at 11:30?

   A: _____

   B: _____

6. he/have lunch at 12:00?

   A: _____

   B: _____

7. Who/eat lunch with him?

   A: _____

   B: _____

8. Where/they/have lunch?

   A: _____

   B: _____

9. Who/he/talk to at 3:30?

   A: _____

   B: _____

10. What/they/discuss?

A: _____

B: _____

3. Statements with the Past Progressive and Simple Past Tense

Read about an explosion at the World Trade Center in New York City.
Complete the story with the past progressive or simple-past-tense form
of the verbs in parentheses ( ).

On February 26, 1993, a bomb

___exploded___ in New York City's
1. (explode)
World Trade Center. At the time, 55,000

people ___were working___ in the Twin
2. (work)
Towers, and thousands of others

_____ the 110-story world-
3. (visit)
famous tourist attraction.

The explosion, which

_____ a little after noon,
4. (take place)

_____ six people and
5. (kill)

_____ more than a thousand
6. (injure)
others. It _____ all day and
7. (take)
half the night to get everyone out of the

building.

When the bomb _____ ,
8. (explode)
the lights _____ , the
9. (go out)
elevators _____ , and fires
10. (stop)
_____ . Many people were in
11. (start)
the wrong place at the wrong time. Four

co-workers _____ lunch in
12. (eat)
their offices when the explosion

_____ the Twin Towers.
13. (shake)
When the blast _____ , walls
14. (occur)
_____ and ceilings
15. (crumble)
_____ . Rescue workers
16. (collapse)

_____ within fifteen
17. (arrive)
minutes and _____ the four
18. (find)
workers dead.

One man _____ in the
19. (walk)
garage beneath the World Trade Center

when the bomb _____ . He
20. (go off)
_____ a heart attack while
21. (have)
rescue workers _____ him to
22. (carry)
the ambulance.

Sixty school children were luckier. They

_____ the huge elevators
23. (ride)
when the lights _____ and
24. (go out)
the elevators _____ . The
25. (stop)
children and their teachers

_____ stand in the hot, dark
26. (have to)
space as they waited for help. Six hours

later, when the elevator

_____ the ground floor, the
27. (reach)
school bus driver _____ for
28. (wait)
them. He _____ the children
29. (drive)
home to their worried families. How did

the children feel while all this

_____ ? "We were scared,"
30. (happen)
they answered.

This is one class trip they will never forget.

4. Questions with the Past Progressive and Simple Past Tense

Reporters are interviewing people about the explosion at the World Trade Center. Use the past progressive and the simple past tense to write the interview questions.

1. What/you do/when you feel the explosion?

   A: *What were you doing when you felt the explosion?*

   B: I was sitting in my chair.

2. What happen/when the bomb explode?

   A: _____

   B: I flew off my chair and landed on the floor.

3. What/the school children do/when the lights/go out?

   A: _____

   B: They were riding the elevator.

4. How many people/work in the building/when the bomb/explode?

   A: _____

   B: Approximately 55,000.

5. Four World Trade Center workers were killed. What/they do/when the bomb/go off?

   A: _____

   B: They were having lunch in their offices.

6. What/happen to the offices/when the blast occur?

   A: _____

   B: The walls crumbled and the ceilings collapsed.

7. There was a man in the garage. What/he do/when the bomb explode?

   A: _____

   B: He was walking to his car.

8. What/happen/when the rescue workers/bring him to the ambulance?

   A: _____

   B: He had a heart attack before they got him in the ambulance.

1. Subject Questions

Ask questions about the words in italics. Use **What, Whose, Who,** *or* **How many**.

1. *Something* happened last night.

   What happened last night?

2. *Someone's* phone rang at midnight.

   _____

3. *Someone* was calling for Megan.

   _____

4. *Someone* was having a party.

   _____

5. *Some number of* people left the party.

   _____

6. *Something* surprised them.

   _____

7. *Someone's* friend called the police.

   _____

8. *Some number of* police arrived.

   _____

8

Wh–Questions: Subject and Predicate

2. Predicate Questions

Use the cues to write questions about Megan Knight, an accountant in Texas.
Then match each question to its correct answer.

QUESTIONS	ANSWERS

1. Where/she/live?

   Where does she live?   _e_

   a. Two years.

2. How many rooms/her apartment/have?

   _____ ____

   b. By bus.

3. How much rent/she/pay?

   _____ ____

   c. The first of the month.

4. When/she/pay the rent?

   _____ ____

   d. Ling, Jackson, & Drew, Inc.

5. Who/she/live with?

   _____ ____

   e. In Texas.

6. What/she/do?

   _____ ____

   f. Five and a half.

7. Which company/she/work for?

   _____ ____

   g. She's an accountant.

8. How long/she/plan to stay there?

   _____ ____

   h. Her sister.

9. How/she/get to work?

   _____ ____

   i. Because she doesn't like to drive.

10. Why/she/take the bus?

   _____ ____

   j. About $500 a month.

3. Subject and Predicate Questions

Megan wrote a letter to her friend, Janice. The letter got wet, and now Janice can't read some parts of it. What questions does Janice ask to get the missing information?

Dear Janice,

Hi! I just moved to _____ .¹ I left Chicago because _____ .² _____ ³ moved with me, and we are sharing an apartment. I got a job in a _____ .⁴ It started _____ .⁵ The people seem nice.

Our apartment is great. It has _____ ⁶ rooms. _____ ⁷ of the rooms came with carpeting, but two of them have beautiful wood floors. The rent isn't too high, either. We each pay $ _____ ⁸ a month.

We need to buy some _____ .⁹ _____ 's ¹⁰ brother wants to visit her, so we really need an extra bed. By the way, _____ ¹¹ called last Sunday. I also spoke to _____ .¹² They want to visit us in _____ .¹³

Would you like to come too? Is that a good time for you? There's plenty of room because _____ .¹⁴ Write and let me know.

Love,
Megan

1. *Where did you move?*

2. _____

3. _____

4. _____

5. _____

6. _____

7. _____

8. _____

9. _____

10. _____

11. _____

12. _____

13. _____

14. _____

PART III: FUTURE

1. Affirmative Statements with *Be Going to*

Read the situations below. Write a prediction. Use **be going to** *and the correct information from the box.*

| crash | get a ticket | make a left turn | ~~Take a trip~~ |
| eat lunch | get gas | rain | wash the car |

1. Mr. Medina is carrying two suitcases toward his car.

   He's going to take a trip.

2. Ms. Marshall has a bucket of water, soap, and a sponge.

   _____

3. Mr. and Mrs. Johnson are driving into an Exxon service station.

   _____

4. Fred is driving behind a woman in a black sports car. The left indicator is

   flashing.

   _____

5. Marcia is driving 70 miles per hour in a 50-mile-per-hour zone. A police

   officer is right behind her.

   _____

6. A blue Ford is driving directly toward a white Toyota. They don't have time

   to stop.

   _____

7. It's noon. The Smiths are driving into a Burger King parking lot.

   _____

8. The sky is full of dark clouds.

   _____

2. Questions with *Be Going to*

Write questions using the cues.

1. What/you/do this summer?

   A: *What are you going to do this summer?*

   B: My wife and I are going to take a trip to San Francisco.

2. How long/you/stay?

   A: _____

   B: Just for a week.

3. you/stay at a hotel?

   A: _____

   B: Yes. We're staying at a hotel in North Beach.

4. What/you/do in San Francisco?

   A: _____

   B: Oh, the usual, I suppose. Sightseeing and shopping.

5. you/visit Fisherman's Wharf?

   A: _____

   B: Yes. We're going to take one of those city bus tours.

6. your daughter/go with you?

   A: _____

   B: No, she's going to attend summer school. Our son isn't going either.

7. What/he/do?

   A: _____

   B: He got a job at Burger King.

8. When/you/leave?

   A: _____

   B: June 11.

   A: Have a good trip.

   B: Thanks

3. Affirmative and Negative Statements with *Be Going to*

Look at Mr. and Mrs. Medina's boarding passes. Then read the sentences below. All of them have incorrect information. Correct the information.

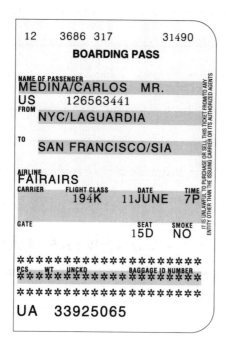

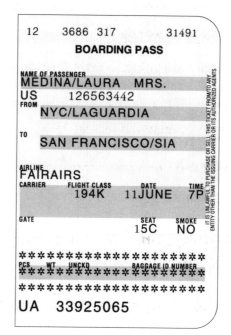

1. Mr. Medina is going to go to Los Angeles.

    He isn't going to go to Los Angeles.

    He's going to go to San Francisco.

2. He's going to take the train.

3. He's going to travel alone.

4. The Medinas are going to leave from Chicago.

5. They're going to fly US Air.

6. They're going to leave on July 11.

_____

_____

7. The plane is going to depart at 7:00 A.M.

_____

_____

8. Mrs. Medina is going to sit in seat 15B.

_____

_____

4. Affirmative and Negative Statements, Questions, and Short Answers with *Will*

*Mrs. Medina is reading the airplane magazine. Complete this magazine interview about personal robots. Use **will** or **won't** and the verbs in parentheses ( ).*

Interviewer: We all know that robots are already working in factories. But tell us something about the

future. _____*Will*_____ people _____*have*_____ robots at home?
1. (have)

Scientist: Yes, they _____. I believe that personal robots _____ as
2.   3.   (become)

common in the home as personal computers are today.

Interviewer: _____ they _____ the computer?
4.   (replace)

Scientist: No, they _____ the computer, but one day robots _____
5.   (replace)

probably _____ computers.
6.   (operate)

Interviewer: Amazing! What other things _____ personal robots _____?
7.   (do)

Scientist: Well, for one thing, they _____ complete home entertainment centers.
8.   (be)

They _____, they _____....
9.   (sing)   10.   (dance)

Interviewer: _____ they _____ jokes?
11.   (tell)

Scientist: Yes, they _____! But, as with humans, they _____ always
12.

_____ funny!
13.   (be)

(Continued on next page.)

Interviewer: What else _____ the personal robot _____?
14. (do)

_____ it _____ more serious uses?
15. (have)

Scientist: Yes, it _____. Robots _____ probably
16.

_____ care for this country's aging population. They
17. (help)

_____ people, but they _____ some of the more routine
18. (replace)   19. (perform)

activities such as vacuuming and loading the dishwasher.

Interviewer: It all sounds great. Do you predict any problems?

Scientist: Unfortunately, yes. Some people _____ happy with the spread of robots.
20. (be)

Not everyone's life _____. Some people _____ their jobs
21. (improve)   22. (lose)

to robots. And other people _____ criminal robots!
23. (create)

Interviewer: _____ we _____ new laws to deal with robotic crime?
24. (need)

Scientist: I'm afraid so.

Interviewer: Tell me, how _____ these personal robots _____?
25. (look)

Scientist: Well, they _____ exactly like humans, but they _____
26. (look)   27. (resemble)

them.

Interviewer: And when _____ all this _____?
28. (happen)

Scientist: Soon! I predict it _____ in the very near future.
29. (happen)

5. Recognizing the Simple Present and Present Progressive When They Refer to the Future

*Read this article about a new play. Underline the simple-present-tense verbs and present progressive verbs **only** when they refer to the future.*

A NEW PLAY
BATS

Next Wednesday <u>is</u> the first performance of **Bats**. Melissa Robins is playing the leading role. Robins, who lives in Italy and who is vacationing in Greece, is not available for an interview at this time. She is, however, appearing on Channel 8's **Theater Talk** sometime next month.

Although shows traditionally begin at 8:00 P.M., **Bats**, because of its length, starts a half-hour earlier.

Immediately following the opening-night performance, the company is having a reception in the theater lounge. Tickets are still available. Call 555–6310 for more information.

6. Contrast of Future Forms

Read the conversations and circle the most appropriate future forms.

1. **A:** What time *do we arrive*/*will we arrive* in San Francisco?

   B: I'm not sure, but here's the schedule.

2. **A:** Why did you bring your computer with you?

   B: *I'll do/I'm going to do* some work while we're away.

3. **A:** I'm thirsty. I think *I'll ask/I'm asking* for a Coke.

   B: Good idea. There's the flight attendant.

4. **A:** Excuse me. Do you know what the weather's like in San Francisco?

   B: It's clear now, but *it's raining/it's going to rain* tomorrow.

5. **A:** Which movie *will they show/are they showing*?

   B: *Rocky 4*. Have you seen it?

(Continued on next page.)

6. **A:** Just look at those dark clouds!

   B: I see. It looks like *we're going to have/we'll have* some rough weather ahead.

7. **A:** I'm tired. I think *I'll take/I'm taking* a little nap. Wake me when the movie begins.

   B: OK. Sweet dreams.

8. **A:** It's 11:00 P.M. already!

   B: I know. *We're going to arrive/We arrive* late.

9. **A:** You know. I don't think the airport buses run after midnight.

   B: I'm afraid you're right. How *are we going to get/are we getting* to the hotel?

10. **A:** Hhmm. No buses. Well, that's no problem. *We'll take/We're going to take* a taxi instead.

    B: Good idea.

11. **A:** I missed the announcement. What did the captain say?

    B: He said, "Fasten your seat belts. *We're landing/We'll land* in about ten minutes."

12. **C:** How long *are you going to stay/will you stay* in San Francisco?

A & B: Just a week.

   C: Well, enjoy yourselves. And thank you for flying FairAirs.

1. Simple Present Tense or Future with Will

Complete the clauses with the correct form of the verbs in parentheses ( ). Then match each time clause to a main clause.

TIME CLAUSE

MAIN CLAUSE

___h___ 1. When the alarm clock

___rings___,
  (ring)

a. they _____ very tired.
          (be)

_____ 2. As soon as the coffee

_____ ready,
  (be)

b. she _____.
          (drive)

_____ 3. When they _____
              (finish)

breakfast,

c. they _____ it.
          (drink)

_____ 4. After her husband

_____ the dishes,
  (wash)

d. they _____ their seat belts.
          (fasten)

_____ 5. As soon as they _____
                (get in)

the car,

e. she _____ them.
          (dry)

_____ 6. Until he _____ his
              (get)

driver's license,

f. they _____ their umbrellas.
          (need)

_____ 7. Until the rain _____,
                (stop)

g. they _____ the dishes.
          (do)

_____ 8. By the time the day

_____ over,
  (be)

h. she _'ll get up_.
          (get up)

2. Simple Present or Future (Will/Be Going to) and Time Expressions

Vera is a student. Look at her future plans. Complete the sentences below with the correct form of the verbs in parentheses ( ) and choose the correct time expression.

Future Plans

Take the TOEFL®* exam
Apply to college for next year
Finish school
Visit Aunt Isabel at Shadybrook
Get a summer job and take a computer-
 programming course
Fly to Brazil — Aug. 28
Get married! — Sept. 30
Return to the United States

*TOEFL® = Test of English as a Foreign Language

1. Vera ____will take____ the TOEFL exam ____before____ she ____applies____ to college.
    (take)   (when/before)   (apply)

2. Vera _____ to college _____ she _____ school.
    (apply)   (before/after)   (finish)

3. _____ she _____ school, she _____ her aunt.
    (Before/After)   (finish)   (visit)

4. _____ she _____ at a summer job, she _____ a course in
    (Before/While)   (work)   (take)
   computer programming.

5. She _____ her aunt _____ she _____ a summer job.
      (visit)   (while/before)   (get)

6. _____ she _____ the computer course, she _____ to Brazil.
    (Before/When)   (finish)   (fly)

7. She _____ _____ she _____ in Brazil.
   (get married)   (when/before)   (be)

8. She _____ to the United States _____ she _____.
   (return)   (before/after)   (get married)

3. Simple Present Tense or Future

Vera's aunt lives at Shadybrook Retirement Village. Complete this ad for
Shadybrook. Use the correct form of the verbs in parentheses ( ).

Shadybrook Retirement Village

What ___*will*___ you ___*do*___ when you _____ ?
                    1. (do)   2. (retire)

Where _____ you _____ when you finally
                              3. (go)

_____ all that free time?
   4. (have)

By the time you _____ 65, you probably _____ to
                     5. (turn)   6. (want)

make some major life changes. Here at *Shadybrook Retirement*

Village, you can enjoy swimming, tennis, golf, and much more.

Come and see for yourself. After you _____ us, you
                                         7. (visit)

_____ to leave!
   8. (not want)

4. Sentence Combining

Combine these sentences. Use the simple present tense and future forms
(will/be going to).

1. Vera will finish her summer job. Then she's going to fly to Brazil.

   ___*Vera is going to fly to Brazil*___ after ___*she finishes her summer job.*___

2. Vera will save enough money from her summer job. Then she's going to buy a plane ticket.

   As soon as _____

3. Vera's going to buy presents for her family. Then she's going to go home.

   Before _____

4. Vera will arrive at the airport. Her father will be there to drive her home.

   When _____

(Continued on next page.)

5. Vera and her father will get home. They'll immediately have dinner.

   As soon as _____

6. They'll finish dinner. Then Vera will give her family the presents.

   _____ after _____

7. Vera's brother will wash the dishes, and Vera's sister will dry them.

   _____ while _____

8. The whole family will stay up talking. Then the clock will strike midnight.

   _____ until _____

9. They'll all feel very tired. Then they'll go to bed.

   By the time _____

10. Vera's head will hit the pillow, and she'll fall asleep immediately.

   _____ as soon as _____

1. Spelling: Regular and Irregular Past Participles

Complete the chart.

BASE FORM	SIMPLE PAST	PAST PARTICIPLE
1. be	was/were	*been*
2. look	looked	_____
3. come	came	_____
4. bring	brought	_____
5. play	played	_____
6. have	had	_____
7. get	got	_____
8. fall	fell	_____
9. watch	watched	_____
10. lose	lost	_____
11. win	won	_____
12. eat	ate	_____

2. For or Since

Put these time expressions in the correct column.

~~1993~~	4:00 P.M.	Monday	a day
yesterday	an hour	she was a child	
a long time	ten years	many months	

FOR	SINCE
_____	*1993*
_____	_____
_____	_____
_____	_____
_____	_____

3. Affirmative Statements with *For* and *Since*

*Complete these brief biographies of famous people. Use the present perfect form of the verbs in parentheses ( ) and choose between **for** and **since**.*

1. **Toni Morrison** (1931–) _____*has been*_____ a novelist _____ more than
     1. (be)   2. (for/since)

   twenty years. Her first novel, *The Bluest Eye*, was published in 1970. _____ then, she
                                                                          3. (For/Since)

   _____ five more novels and _____ work on another one. She
     4. (write)   5. (begin)

   _____ a professor at Princeton University _____ 1987.
     6. (be)   7. (for/since)

   In 1988, Morrison won the Pulitzer Prize for Fiction for her novel, *Beloved*, a powerful work

   about the experience of African-American women after the Civil War. In 1993, she won the world's

   highest literary honor—the Nobel Prize for Literature. She is the first African-American to win this

   award. It is also the first time the award _____ to an American woman
                                               8. (go)

   _____ 1938.
     9. (for/since)

2. **Jodie Foster** (1962–) _____ an actress _____ most of her
                                1. (be)   2. (for/since)

   life. At the age of three, she began appearing in television commercials. She made her first movie in

   1972 and _____ in dozens of movies _____ then. In 1985, she
              3. (appear)   4. (for/since)

   graduated with honors from Yale University. _____ her graduation, she
                                                 5. (For/Since)

   _____ two Oscars for Best Actress, _____ her first film, and
     6. (receive)   7. (direct)

   _____ her own production company, called Egg Pictures.
     8. (form)

3. Jonathan Knight, Jordan Knight, Joe McIntyre, Donnie Wahlberg, and Danny Wood, members

   of **The New Kids on the Block** (1984–), _____ the most successful pop music
                                                 1. (be)

   group in the United States _____ the last ten years. In 1986, their first single record,
                               2. (for/since)

   "Be My Girl," reached the U.S. Top 10. _____ then, they _____ more
                                            3. (For/Since)   4. (have)

   than eight U.S. Top 10 entries and _____ videos that _____ over a
                                        5. (make)   6. (sell)

   million copies each. In 1989, the five teenagers were the top recording act in the United States.

   _____ 1990, they _____ very famous in Great Britain, too, where they
     7. (For/Since)   8. (become)

   scored seven Top 10 singles—the first American group ever to do that.

4. Questions and Answers

Ask and answer questions about the people in Exercise 3.

BIOGRAPHY 1

1. How long/Toni Morrison/be a novelist?

   A: *How long has Toni Morrison been a novelist?*

   B: *She's been a novelist for more than twenty years.*

2. How many novels/she/write since 1970?

   A: _____

   B: _____

3. she/receive any awards since her Pulitzer Prize for Fiction?

   A: _____

   B: _____

BIOGRAPHY 2

4. How long/Jodie Foster/be an actress?

   A: _____

   B: _____

5. she/win any Oscars since 1985?

   A: _____

   B: _____

6. she/direct any movies since she graduated from Yale?

   A: _____

   B: _____

BIOGRAPHY 3

7. The New Kids on the Block/be/a pop music group for more than twenty years?

   A: _____

   B: _____

8. How long/they/be successful in the United States?

   A: _____

   B: _____

(Continued on next page.)

9. they/have any Top 10 entries since their first U.S. hit?

A: _____

B: _____

5. Affirmative and Negative Statements

Read the pairs of sentences. Write a third sentence that has a meaning similar to the two sentences.

1. Carlos became a tennis player in 1959.

+ He is still a tennis player. _____

= *Carlos has been a tennis player since 1959.* _____

2. Fei-Mei competed in 1992.

+ That was the last time she competed. _____

= *Fei-Mei hasn't competed since 1992.* _____

3. Min Ho won two awards in 1993.

+ He won another award in 1994. _____

= _____ since 1992.

4. Marilyn appeared in a movie in 1989.

+ She appeared in another movie last year. _____

= _____ since 1988.

5. Victor saw Marilyn in 1989.

+ That was the last time he saw her. _____

= _____

6. Andreas lost two games in February of this year.

+ He lost another game last week. _____

= _____ since January of this year.

1. Spelling: Regular and Irregular Past Participles

Complete the chart.

BASE FORM	SIMPLE PAST	PAST PARTICIPLE
1. become	became	*become*
2. act	acted	_____
3. give	gave	_____
4. keep	kept	_____
5. hold	held	_____
6. travel	traveled	_____
7. sing	sang	_____
8. dance	danced	_____
9. fight	fought	_____
10. know	knew	_____
11. drink	drank	_____
12. smile	smiled	_____

Present Perfect:
Already and Yet

2. Questions and Statements with Already and Yet

Monica Clarke is a home health aide. Read her list of things to do. She has checked (√) all the things she's already done. Ask and answer questions about the words in parentheses ( ).

Monday. March 29

- ☑ make breakfast for pt.
- ☐ make lunch for pt.
- ☑ take pt.'s temperature
- ☐ give pt. a bath
- ☑ change pt.'s bandages
- ☑ go food shopping
- ☐ do the laundry
- ☐ call doctor for the blood-test results
- ☐ exercise pt.'s legs
- ☑ give pt. medication

---

1. (breakfast) *Has she made breakfast for the patient yet?*

   She's already made breakfast for the patient.

2. (lunch) *Has she made lunch for the patient yet?*

   She hasn't made lunch for the patient yet.

3. (food shopping) _____

   _____

4. (medication) _____

   _____

5. (doctor) _____

   _____

6. (bandages) _____

   _____

7. (bath) _____

_____

8. (temperature) _____

_____

9. (laundry) _____

_____

10. (legs) _____

_____

3. Correct the Mistakes

Monica wrote a letter to a friend, but she made five mistakes in the use of the present perfect with **already** *and* **yet**. *Find the mistakes and correct them.*

Dear Suzanne,

It's 8:00 P.M. and I'm exhausted. I'm at my
new job. I've already ~~work~~ worked here for two weeks.
The job is hard, but I feel that the patient have
already made progress. She hasn't walked
already, but she's already sat up by herself.
She can feed herself now, too. Already she has
gained three pounds.

How are you? When are you coming to visit?
Have you decide yet? Please write.

Love,
Monica

13

Present Perfect: Indefinite Past

1. Spelling: Regular and Irregular Past Participles

Complete the chart.

BASE FORM	SIMPLE PAST	PAST PARTICIPLE
1. work	worked	*worked*
2. begin	began	_____
3. forgive	forgave	_____
4. promise	promised	_____
5. go	went	_____
6. feel	felt	_____
7. grow	grew	_____
8. hear	heard	_____
9. see	saw	_____
10. decide	decided	_____
11. keep	kept	_____
12. act	acted	_____

2. Affirmative and Negative Statements

Every year Hollywood gives out awards for movie achievements. Complete this editorial about the Academy Awards. Use the present-perfect form of the verbs in parentheses ( ).

It's Oscar night once again. You and a billion other people from ninety countries around the world _____ *have* _____ just _____ *turned on* _____ your TVs to
1. (turn on)
see who Hollywood will honor this year. The Academy of Motion Picture Arts and Sciences _____ nominees
2. (choose)
to compete in categories including Best Picture, Best Actor, Best Actress, and Best Director. Actors and actresses from around the world _____ to
3. (come)
Hollywood to take part in the gala event.

As always, opinions of the nominations _____ mixed.
4. (be)
Many groups are unhappy. Lately, there _____ many great roles
5. (not be)
for women. In fact, there

_____ seldom

_____ a Hollywood
6. (be)
actress who _____ past
7. (work)
the age of 45. "I _____

recently _____ several
8. (read)
scripts," said one well-known actress,

"and I _____ all of them.
9. (rejected)
The stories are ridiculous." This absence of good roles for women may partly explain why out of more than 2,000 Oscar awards fewer than 300

_____ to women.
10. (go)
African-American actors and actresses

_____ also

_____ excluded. Fewer
11. (feel)
than ten _____ awards for
12. (get)
acting.

Actors and actresses with physical disabilities _____ major
13. (not get)
roles either. Many movies

_____ recently

_____ the stories of
14. (tell)
people who are blind or paralyzed, but

"able-bodied" Hollywood stars

_____ these parts.
15. (play)
On screen as well as off, we still have a long way to go toward equal opportunity. In the meantime, Hollywood

_____ another evening of
16. (produce)
glitter and glamour as movies continue to fascinate and entertain us. As one actor said, "They take us to places we

_____ never

_____ and allow us to see
17. (be)
things we _____

never_____ .
18. (see)
So, relax, have some popcorn, and enjoy the show.

3. Questions

Bob Waters is interviewing a movie star. Read the star's answers. Write Bob's questions.

1. **Bob:** *How many movies have you been in?*

   Star: I've been in ten movies.

2. **Bob:** _____

   Star: I've received four nominations for Best Actor.

3. **Bob:** Some actors don't like to see their own films.

   _____

   Star: No, I haven't. I've never watched the completed films.

4. **Bob:** _____

   Star: No, never. I've never gone to the Academy Awards. I prefer to watch the event on TV.

5. **Bob:** Your last movie was an Italian production.

   _____

   Star: I've acted in foreign films three times.

6. **Bob:** _____

   Star: Yes, I have. I've worked with Sophia Loren once.

7. **Bob:** You've made a lot of money in a very short time.

   _____

   Star: How? It's changed my life in many ways. I've traveled more, I've bought a new house…

8. **Bob:** _____

   Star: No, I haven't. I haven't read any good scripts lately. But I'm sure a good one will come my

   way soon.

1. Present Perfect or Simple Past Tense

Complete the chart about Joe Dorsey, a teacher who is looking for a job.

	LAST YEAR	THIS YEAR
1.	Joe answered twenty employment ads.	*Joe has answered* thirty ads.
2.	_____ two job interviews.	Joe has had three job interviews.
3.	_____ one job offer.	Joe has gotten three job offers.
4.	Joe made $18,000.	_____ the same amount of money.
5.	Joe was sick once.	_____ sick twice.
6.	_____ well.	Joe has looked tired.
7.	_____ a new camera.	Joe has bought a VCR.
8.	Joe paid with cash.	_____ by credit card.
9.	Joe read five books.	_____ two books.
10.	_____ discouraged.	Joe has felt more encouraged.

Contrast:
Present
Perfect and
Simple Past
Tense

2. Present Perfect or Simple Past Tense

A journalist is interviewing a woman about marriage. Complete the interview with the correct form of the verbs in parentheses ( ).

Interviewer: How long _____*have*_____ you _____*been*_____ married?
1. (be)

Woman: Let's see. We _____ married in 1993, so we _____
2. (get)   3. (be)
married for just a few years.

Interviewer: And, when _____ you _____ your first child?
4. (have)

Woman: Well, I _____ a mother pretty quickly. We _____
5. (become)   6. (have)
Stephanie ten months after we _____ married.
7. (be)

(Continued on next page.)

Interviewer: You say this isn't your first marriage. How long _____ your first marriage

_____?
8. (last)

Woman: About two years. We _____ in 1985.
9. (divorce)

Interviewer: _____ you _____ any kids?
10. (have)

Woman: No, we _____.
11.

Interviewer: Do you still see your first husband?

Woman: Yes. We _____ friends. In fact, I _____ him last week. He and Joe
12. (remain)   13. (see)

_____ friends, too.
14. (become)

Interviewer: _____ he _____?
15. (remarry)

Woman: No, he _____.
16.

Interviewer: In your opinion, why _____ your first marriage _____?
17. (fail)

Woman: I think that we _____ married too young. We _____ each other well
18. (get)   19. (not know)

enough.

Interviewer: Where _____ you _____ Joe?
20. (meet)

Woman: In Atlanta. We _____ both students there.
21. (be)

Interviewer: And when _____ you _____ to Los Angeles?
22. (move)

Woman: This year. Los Angeles is the third city we _____ in! Joe teaches college, and it's
23. (live)

hard to find a permanent job these days.

---

3. | Present Perfect or Simple Past Tense

Read some facts about the changing American family. Complete the state-
ments. Use the correct form of the verbs in the boxes.

begin	~~change~~	get	have

The American family ___*has changed*___ a lot in the past thirty-five years. In the 1960s,
1.

couples _____ to get married at an older age. They also _____ divorced
2.   3.

more frequently than they ever did and _____ fewer children.
4.

be	create	occur	rise

AGE

In 1960, the average age for marriage for women _____ 20.3 and for men, 22.8.

5.

Today it _____ to 24.1 for women and 26.3 for men. In the early 1960s, most divorces

6.

_____ among couples older than 45. Today people of all ages are getting divorced at

7.

a rate of more than 50 percent. This, in part, _____ many single-parent homes.

8.

be	begin	have	increase

BIRTH RATE

In the mid-1960s, birth rates _____ to drop. Then, almost 60 percent of women

9.

_____ three or more children by the time they _____ in their late thirties.

10.   11.

These days, 35 percent of women in the same age group have only two children. In addition, the

number of births to older women _____ greatly _____.

                  12.

change	get	stay

LIVING ARRANGEMENTS

Before 1960, most children _____ in their parents' homes until they

13.

_____ married. This pattern _____ since then. Today many single

14.   15.

people live alone.

4. Correct the Mistakes

Read this student's letter to a friend. There are seven mistakes in the use of the present perfect and the simple past tense. Find and correct them.

> Dear Jennifer,
>
>   Last month I ~~have met~~ *met* the most wonderful guy. His name is Roger, and he is a student in my night class. He lived here since 1992. Before that he lived in Detroit too, so we have a lot in common. Roger has been married for five years but got divorced last April.
>
>   Roger and I spent a lot of time together. Last week I saw him every night, and this week we've already gotten together three times after class. Monday night we have seen a great movie. Did you see *The Purple Room?* It's playing at all the theaters.
>
>   We decided to take a trip back to Detroit in the summer. Maybe we can get together? It would be great to see you again. Please let me know if you'll be there.
>
>   Love,
>   Diana

1. Affirmative Statements with *For* and *Since*

Read the information about a married couple, Pete and Amanda Kelly. Write a sentence that summarizes the information.

1. The year is 1995. Pete and Amanda Kelly moved to New York in 1992. They are still living there.

   They have been living in New York since 1992/for three years.

2. Amanda began work at the *Daily News* in 1994. She's still working there.

   _____

3. Amanda is writing articles about the homeless. She began a series last month.

   _____

4. The number of homeless Americans is increasing. It began to increase steadily in 1980.

   _____

5. Pete is working at a homeless shelter. He started last month.

   _____

6. Pete went back to school last year. He's studying economics.

   _____

7. Amanda and Pete started looking for a new apartment two months ago. They are still looking.

   _____

2. Affirmative and Negative Statements

Complete the statements. Use the present-perfect-progressive form of the verbs in the box.

eat	rain	~~rub~~	study	wait
feel	run	sleep	try	work

1. Amanda's eyes are red. She _____ *'s been rubbing* _____ them all morning.

2. She's tired. She _____ well lately.

3. She's losing weight. She _____ much lately.

(Continued on next page.)

4. Pete is exhausted too. He _____ all night for a test.

5. Amanda doesn't know many people at the *Daily News*. She _____ there very long.

6. She just looked out the window. The street is wet. It _____.

7. Pete is out of breath. He _____.

8. He's only five minutes late. Amanda _____ very long.

9. They're going to look at an apartment. They _____ to find one for months.

10. It's very hard to find an apartment in New York. They're often too expensive. Amanda and Pete _____ very hopeful.

3. Questions with *How Long*

*Look at the picture. Ask questions about the man on the bench, the woman with the dog, the children, the police officer, the two men, and the weather. Begin with **How long** and use the present perfect progressive.*

1. *How long has the man been sitting* _____ on the bench?

2. _____ under the tree?

3. _____ the dog?

4. _____ ball?

5. _____ it _____?

6. _____ the bus?

U N I T

16

Contrast:
Present Perfect
and Present
Perfect
Progressive

▼

1. Present Perfect or Present Perfect Progressive

Read this information about a famous British businesswoman and environmentalist. Complete it with the present perfect or present perfect progressive form of the verbs in parentheses ( ). If either form is possible, use the present perfect progressive.

In a short period of time, Anita Roddick _____*has become*_____ one
1. (become)
of the most successful businesswomen in the world. She is the owner of an

international chain of stores that sells soaps, makeup, body lotions, and

creams. For almost twenty years, The Body Shop _____
2. (sell)
products that are "environmentally friendly." They are made mostly of natural

products from renewable sources, and they come in biodegradable, recyclable

containers. In addition, Roddick, who _____ for years
3. (fight)
against the practice of animal testing of cosmetics, refuses to use any animals

in the testing of her products.

The first Body Shop opened in Brighton, England, in 1976. Since then,

more than 700 stores in more than forty different countries around the world

_____. Roddick relies on the reputation of her products
4. (open)
and stores to attract customers. She _____ never

_____ any advertisements or commercials for her
5. (do)
stores. Lately, however, you *will* see Roddick's face if you turn on your TV. She

_____ on commercials for the American Express charge
6. (appear)
card.

Roddick spends almost half of her time traveling. Right now she is "on the

road." For the past several months, she _____ around
7. (travel)
the world in search of new ideas for her body-care products.

Roddick is more than a businesswoman. She _____
8. (receive)
several awards, including the United Nations Global 500 environmental award.

She is also concerned with human rights, and she _____
9. (start)
a London newspaper that is sold by homeless people.

(Continued on next page.)

Roddick _____ an autobiography, called *Body and Soul: Profits with*
　　　　　　　　10. (write)
Principles. Published in 1991, the book shows how Roddick _____ successfully

_____ business with social responsibility.
　　　11. (combine)

2. Present Perfect or Present Perfect Progressive

Complete this conversation between two friends. Use the present perfect or present perfect progressive
form of the verbs in parentheses ( ).

A: Hi. I ___*haven't seen*___ you around lately. How _____ you
　　　　　1. (not see)

_____?
　　2. (be)

B: OK, thanks. What about you?

A: Not bad. What _____ you _____?
　　　　　　　　　　　　　　　　　　　3. (do)

B: Nothing special. What about you?

A: I _____ a book for this business course I'm taking. It's called *Body and Soul*. It's
　　　　4. (read)

pretty interesting. I can lend it to you when I'm done, if you'd like.

B: Who's it by?

A: Anita Roddick. _____ you ever _____ anything about her?
　　　　　　　　　　　　　　　　　5. (read)

B: Yes. I _____ a few articles about her in the paper.
　　　　　6. (see)

A: _____ you ever _____ any of her products?
　　　　　　　　　　　　　　　7. (buy)

B: As a matter of fact, I _____ her products for years.
　　　　　　　　　　　8. (use)

A: Oh. Where do you buy them?

B: A new shop _____ just _____ on Broadway.
　　　　　　　　　　　　　　　9. (open)

A: Wow, they _____ everywhere, haven't they? I wonder where the next one is going
　　　　　　10. (open)

to be.

3. Questions: Present Perfect or Present Perfect Progressive

Use the cues to write questions about Anita Roddick.

1. she/sell/cosmetics for a long time?

   Has she been selling cosmetics for a long time?

2. How much money/her business/make this year?

   _____

3. How long/she/travel around the world?

   _____

4. How many countries/she/visit?

   _____

5. How many copies of her book/she/sell?

   _____

6. she/write/any books since *Body and Soul*?

   _____

7. she/ever appear on TV?

   _____

8. How long/she and her husband/live in England?

   _____

PART V: ADJECTIVES AND ADVERBS

1. Spelling

Complete the chart.

ADJECTIVES	ADVERBS
1. quick	*quickly*
2. _____	nicely
3. fast	_____
4. good	_____
5. _____	dangerously
6. beautiful	_____
7. _____	hard
8. safe	_____
9. _____	occasionally
10. _____	happily
11. _____	suddenly
12. careful	_____
13. angry	_____
14. _____	unfortunately

2. Word Order

Betty is telling her friend about her new apartment. Put the words in the correct order to make sentences and complete the conversation.

A: Congratulations! (heard about/I/apartment/new/your).

1. *I heard about your new apartment.* _____

B: Thank you! (news/good/fast/travels)!

2. _____

A: What's it like?

B: (five/rooms/has/it/large),

3. _____

and (building/it's/large/a/very/in).

4. _____

A: How's the rent?

B: (too/it's/bad/not).

5. _____

A: And what about the neighborhood?

B: (seems/quiet/it/pretty).

6. _____

But (landlord/the/very/speaks/loudly).

7. _____

A: How come?

B: (well/doesn't/he/hear).

8. _____

A: Well, that doesn't really matter. (it/decision/was/hard/a)?

9. _____

B: Not really. We liked the apartment, and besides (quickly/had to/we/decide).

10. _____

There were a lot of other people interested in it.

A: Oh, no! Look at the time! (I/leave/now/have to).

11. _____

(luck/with/good/apartment/new/your)!

12. _____

B: Thanks. So long.

3. Adjective or Adverb

Betty wrote a letter to a friend. Complete the letter. Use the correct form of the words in parentheses ( ).

Dear Matilda,

    I'm ___totally___ exhausted! Dan and I finished moving into our
        1. (total)

new apartment today. It was a lot of _____ work, but
                            2. (hard)

everything worked out _____ .
                      3. (good)

    The apartment looks _____ . It's _____
                   4. (nice)   5. (extreme)

_____ . The only problem is with the heat. I always feel
6. (comfortable)

_____ . We'll have to speak to the landlord about it. He seems
   7. (cold)

_____ _____ .
  8. (pretty)   9. (friendly)

    People tell me that the neighborhood is very _____ . That's
                             10. (safe)

_____ _____ because I get home _____ from
  11. (real)   12. (important)   13. (late)

work. I hate it when the streets are _____ _____ as
               14. (complete)   15. (empty)

they were in our old neighborhood. Shopping is _____ , too. We
                     16. (good)

can get to all the stores very _____ . The bus stop is
              17. (easy)

_____ the apartment, and the buses run _____ .
  18. (near)   19. (frequently)

    Why don't you come for a visit? It would be _____ to see
                       20. (wonderful)

you. I haven't seen you since our wedding. Please write.

                Love,
                Betty

4.   —ED or —ING Adjectives

Betty and Dan are going to rent a video. Circle the correct adjective form to complete these brief movie reviews from a video guide.

 ━━━━━━━━━━━━━━━━━━━━━━━━━━━━━━━

BILLY BUDD   Based on Herman Melville's powerful and (1. fascinated / fascinating) novel, this well-acted, well-produced film will leave you (2. disturbed / disturbing).

THE BURNING   There's nothing (3. entertained / entertaining) about this 1981 horror film that takes place in a summer camp. You'll be (4. disgusted / disgusting) by all the blood in this story of revenge.

CHARIOTS OF FIRE   Made in England, this is an (5. inspired / inspiring) story about two Olympic runners. Wonderfully acted.

COMING HOME   Jon Voight plays the role of a (6. paralyzed / paralyzing) war veteran in this (7. moved / moving) drama about the effects of war. Powerful.

THE COMPETITION   Well-acted love story about two pianists who fall in love while competing for the top prize in a concert. You'll be (8. moved / moving). Beautiful music.

FOLLOW ME QUIETLY   A (9. frightened / frightening) thriller about a mentally (10. disturbed / disturbing) man who kills people when it rains. Not for the weak-hearted.

THE GREEN WALL   Mario Robles Godoy's photography is (11. astonished / astonishing) in this story of a young Peruvian family. In Spanish with English subtitles.

INVASION OF THE BODY SNATCHERS   One of the most (12. frightened / frightening) science fiction movies ever made. You won't be (13. bored / boring).

WEST SIDE STORY   No matter how many times you see this classic musical, you'll never be (14. disappointed / disappointing). The story, based on Shakespeare's *Romeo and Juliet*, is (15. touched / touching), and the music by Leonard Bernstein is delightful and (16. excited / exciting).

WILBUR AND ORVILLE: THE FIRST TO FLY
This is an (17. entertained / entertaining) biography of the two famous Wright brothers. Good for kids, too. They'll learn a lot without ever being (18. bored / boring).

━━━━━━━━━━━━━━━━━━━━━━━━━━━━━ ★ ☆ ☆

18

Adjectives:
Equatives and
Comparatives

1. Spelling: Regular and Irregular Comparatives

Complete the chart.

ADJECTIVE	COMPARATIVE
1. slow	*slower*
2. expensive	
3. hot	
4. big	
5. good	
6. difficult	
7. pretty	
8. beautiful	
9. bad	
10. long	
11. far	
12. careful	
13. dangerous	
14. early	

2. The Comparative Form

*Complete this conversation between two neighbors who meet in a department store. Use the correct form of the words in parentheses ( ). Use **than** when necessary.*

Betty: Mia!

Mia: Betty! What are you doing here?

Betty: I'm trying to buy a microwave oven. Do you know if the small ones are

really any __*worse than*__ the _____ ones?
          1. (bad)   2. (large)

Mia: I'm not sure, but I think they're _____. Are you getting things
                                      3. (slow)

for your new apartment?

Betty: Yes. Dan and I moved in last Friday.

Mia: How do you like it?

Betty: It's great. It's _____ our old one. It has an extra bedroom. And it faces the back, so
               4. (big)

    it's _____. You can't hear the traffic at all.
        5. (quiet)

Mia: How's the rent?

Betty: That's the only problem. It's a little _____.
                           6. (expensive)

Mia: But it's _____ a house.
        7. (cheap)

Betty: That's true. The location is _____ for us, too. Everything is _____
                       8. (good)   9. (convenient)

    —shopping, schools.

Mia: Isn't it _____ from your office, though?
        10. (far)

Betty: Yes. But I take the express bus and get there even _____ before. Besides, I can relax
                                  11. (fast)

    on the bus, so it's really _____.
                12. (comfortable)

3. The Comparative Form

*Look at this chart comparing two microwave ovens. Complete the sentences,
using the words in parentheses ( ). Also, fill in the blanks with the brand—**X** or **Y**.*

				Better ⟷ Worse			
Brand	Price	Size (cubic ft.)	Weight (lbs.)	Defrosting	Heating	Speed	Noise
X	$181	0.5	31	●	○	◐	○
Y	$147	0.6	36	◐	●	●	◐

1. Brand ___X___ is ___*more expensive than*___ Brand ___*Y*___.
                      (expensive)

2. Brand _____ is _____ Brand _____.
                      (cheap)

3. Brand _____ is _____ Brand _____.
                      (large)

4. Brand _____ is _____ Brand _____.
                      (heavy)

5. For defrosting food, Brand _____ is _____ Brand _____.
                                    (efficient)

6. For heating food, Brand _____ is _____ Brand _____.
                              (effective)

7. Brand _____ is _____ Brand _____.
                      (fast)

(Continued on next page.)

8. Brand _____ is _____ Brand _____.

(noisy)

9. In general, Brand _____ seems _____ Brand _____.

(good)

10. In general, Brand _____ seems _____ Brand _____.

(bad)

4. Comparisons with As...As

Read the facts about Los Angeles and New York City. Complete the sentences.
Use the words in parentheses ( ) with **as...as** *or* **not as...as.**

	LOS ANGELES	NEW YORK CITY
Population	3,485,398	7,322,564
Land area	467.4 square miles	321.8 square miles
Average temperature	57.2°F (January)	31.8°F (January)
	74.1°F (July)	76.7°F (July)
Sunny days	143	107
Annual rainfall	12"	40"
Wind speed	7.4 mph	9.4 mph

1. In population, Los Angeles is _____*not as big as*_____ New York.

(big)

2. In land area, New York is _____ Los Angeles.

(big)

3. In the winter, Los Angeles is _____ New York.

(cold)

4. In the summer, Los Angeles is almost _____ New York.

(hot)

5. Los Angeles is _____ New York.

(wet)

6. Los Angeles is _____ New York.

(windy)

7. New York is _____ Los Angeles.

(sunny)

5. Cause and Effect with Two Comparatives

Research suggests that there is a connection between the crime rate in U.S. cities and certain other factors. Read the information. Rewrite the information, using two comparatives.

1. When cities are large, they usually have high crime rates.

   The larger the city, the higher the crime rate.

2. When cities are small, they usually have low crime rates.

   _____

3. When cities have warm climates, the police are usually busy.

   _____

4. When the weather is cold, there is usually a great number of robberies.

   _____

5. When the police force is large, the city is usually violent.

   _____

6. When it's late in the day, the number of car thefts is usually high.

   _____

7. When the unemployment rate is high, the crime rate is usually also high.

   _____

8. When the population is mobile (people move from place to place), the city is usually dangerous.

   _____

9. When communities are organized, neighborhoods are usually safe.

   _____

6. The Comparative to Express Change

*Look at these graphs. They show trends in the capital of the United States,
Washington, D.C. Make statements about the trends. Use the comparative
form of the adjectives in parentheses ( ).*

1. Population

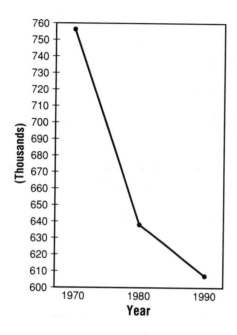

The population of Washington, D.C., _____*is getting smaller and smaller.*
                                            (small)

2. Population Per Square Mile

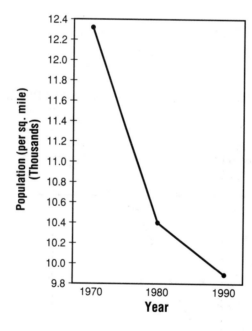

Washington, D.C., _____
                                    (crowded)

3. Unemployment

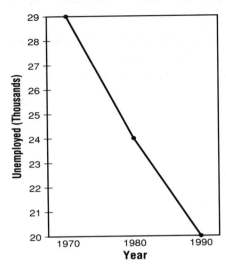

The number of unemployed people _____
                                                    (low)

4. Personal Income

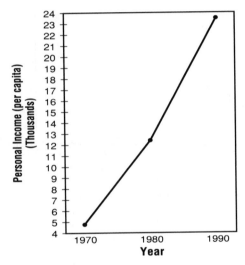

Personal income _____
                                    (high)

5. Average House Price

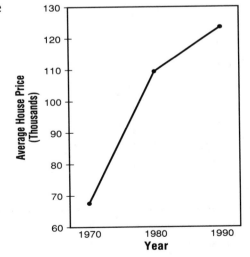

Homes _____
                    (expensive)

(Continued on next page.)

6. Motor Vehicle Deaths

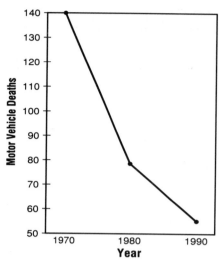

The roads in Washington, D.C., _____

(dangerous)

7. Violent Crimes (per 100,000 people)

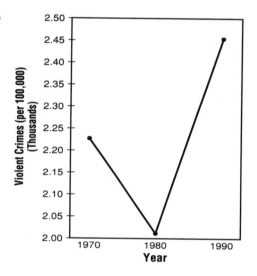

Since 1980, life in Washington, D.C., _____

(violent)

8. Number of Prisoners

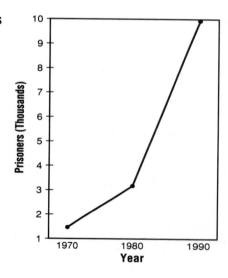

The prisons _____

(crowded)

1. Spelling: Regular and Irregular Superlatives

Complete the chart.

ADJECTIVES	SUPERLATIVE
1. nice	*the nicest*
2. funny	
3. big	
4. wonderful	
5. good	
6. bad	
7. happy	
8. important	
9. warm	
10. interesting	
11. far	
12. intelligent	
13. slow	
14. expensive	

Adjectives: Superlatives ▼

2. The Superlative

*Look at the newspaper ads for three cameras and complete the conversation between a customer and salesclerk. Use the superlative form (**the...–est** or **the most/the least**)of the adjectives in parentheses ( ). Also, write the name of the camera they are talking about.*

Low Price of $49⁹⁸

 **RIKON**

• Compact 35mm • Built-in Flash with red-eye reduction • Focus-Free • Auto Film Loading • Auto Advance • Auto Exposure

$39⁹⁸  *FUNJI*

• Focus-Free 35mm with film and batteries • Focus-Free operation • Motorized Auto Advance • Built-in Flash • Drop-in Loading

 **MINON**

~~$129⁹⁸~~ $99⁹⁸

• Special One-Time Offer • 35–60mm Zoom Lens • Auto Focus • Built-in Automatic Flash • Ultra Compact — Fits in Your Pocket • Weighs 14 oz.

(Continued on next page.)

Clerk: Can I help you?

Customer: Yes. I'm looking for a camera for my daughter. I want to spend between $50.00 and

$100.00. What's _____*the best*_____ camera you have in that price range?
1. (good)

Clerk: Well, there are three cameras I can show you. _____ is the
2. (expensive)

_____ . It sells for only $39.98.
3.

Customer: And how much is _____?
4. (expensive)

Clerk: That's the _____. It's on sale for $99.98, and I can guarantee that
5.

that's _____ price in town. It usually sells for $130.00.
6. (low)

Customer: How are the three cameras different?

Clerk: Well, the _____ is _____. It can fit right inside
7.   8. (small)

your pocket.

Customer: That sounds good. I guess it's _____, too.
9. (light)

Clerk: No, not really. It's the only one of the three with a zoom lens. That makes it

_____ because it brings the picture closer to you. But it also makes
10. (powerful)

the camera _____. It weighs 14 ounces. The other two weigh only
11. (heavy)

10 ounces.

Customer: I see. What about flashes?

Clerk: All three come with a built-in flash. But the _____ turns on automat-
12.

ically when there isn't enough light. That makes it _____. Oh, you
13. (convenient)

should also know about a special feature of the _____. It has
14.

what's called "red-eye reduction." That means that when you take a picture of a person

and use the flash, the person's eyes won't look red. That's often a problem when you use

a flash.

Customer: Oh, that's probably _____ feature in my daughter's case. She only
15. (important)

takes pictures of flowers and trees!

3. The Superlative

Complete these world facts. Use the superlative form of the correct adjectives from the box.

busy	far	~~large~~	popular	small
expensive	fast	long	slow	tall

1. Russia is 6,592,800 square miles. It's _____ *the largest* _____ country in the world.

2. The Republic of Maldives is only 114 square miles. It's _____ country in the world.

3. The Sears Tower in Chicago has 110 floors. It's _____ building in the world.

4. The Seikan Tunnel in Japan stretches for 33.1 miles. It's _____ tunnel in the world.

5. The planet Pluto is 3,666 million miles from the Sun. It's _____ planet from the Sun.

6. In one year, O'Hare airport in Chicago serves almost 60,000,000 passengers. It's _____ airport in the world.

7. More Americans visit Mexico than any other country. It's _____ vacation destination for people from the United States.

8. The cheetah (an animal in the cat family) runs 70 mph. It's _____ animal in the world.

9. The garden snail moves at a speed of only 0.03 mph. It's _____ animal in the world.

10. It costs more than $16,000 a year to go to Bennington College in Vermont. It's _____ college in the United States.

1. Spelling: Regular and Irregular Comparative and Superlative Forms of Adverbs

Complete the chart.

ADVERB	COMPARATIVE	SUPERLATIVE
1. quickly	*more quickly*	*the most quickly*
2. fast		
3. beautifully		
4. soon		
5. dangerously		
6. well		
7. early		
8. carefully		
9. badly		
10. far		

2. The Comparative Form of Adverbs

*Here is what basketball players from two teams said about the game they played. Complete their comments. Use the correct form of the words in parentheses ( ). Use **than** when necessary.*

George: The other team played well, but we played much

_____*better*_____. That's why we got the results we did.
　　　　　1. (good)

* *

Bob: We played _____ our opponents. We deserved
　　　　　　　　　　　2. (hard)

to win, and we did.

* *

Alex: It wasn't a great game for me. I moved _____
　　　　　　　　　　　　　　　　　　　　　　　　3. (slow)

usual because of my bad ankle. In a few weeks I should be able to

run _____. I hope that'll help the team.
　　　　4. (fast)

* *

Rick: Our shooting was off today. We missed too many baskets. We need to shoot

_____ if we want to win.
       5. (accurate)

****

Larry: I was surprised by how well they played. They played _____ they've
       6. (aggressive)

played in a long time. We couldn't beat them.

****

Elvin: I'm disappointed. We've been playing a lot _____ our opponents this
       7. (bad)

season. We really have to concentrate _____ in order to break this
       8. (good)

losing streak.

****

Randy: Team spirit was very strong. We played a lot _____ together, and it
       9. (successful)

paid off.

****

Dennis: Of course I'm happy with the results. But if we want to keep it up, we have to practice

_____ and _____ we have been. I think we got
    10. (serious)   11. (regular)

lucky today.

Now write the names of the players under the correct team.

WINNING TEAM

George

_____

_____

_____

LOSING TEAM

_____

_____

_____

_____

3. Comparison of Adverbs with As...As

Look at these track-and-field records for four athletes. Then complete the statements about them. Use the cues and (not) as...as.

EVENT	100 METER RUN	HIGH JUMP	DISCUS THROW
Athlete A	9 min. 86 sec.	7 ft. 9-¾ in.	217 ft. 2 in.
Athlete B	10 min. 02 sec.	6 ft. 8-¼ in.	233 ft.
Athlete C	9 min. 99 sec.	7 ft. 10 in.	220 ft. 6 in.
Athlete D	10 min. 02 sec.	7 ft. 10 in.	233 ft.
Athlete E	10 min. 18 sec.	7 ft. 11 in.	233 ft. 1 in.

1. Athlete B ___*didn't run as fast as*___ Athlete A.
   (run/fast)

2. Athlete B _____ Athlete D.
   (run/fast)

3. Athlete C _____ Athlete D.
   (jump/high)

4. Athlete A _____ Athlete E.
   (jump/high)

5. Athlete C _____ Athlete E.
   (throw the discus/far)

6. Athlete D _____ Athlete B.
   (throw the discus/far)

7. All in all, Athlete B _____ Athlete D.
   (do/good)

8. All in all, Athlete A _____ Athlete C.
   (compete/successful)

4. The Comparative and the Superlative of Adverbs

Look at the chart in Exercise 3. Complete the statements with the correct form of the words in parentheses ( ). Use than when necessary. Fill in the blanks with the correct athlete—A, B, C, D, or E.

1. Athlete B ran ___*faster than*___ Athlete __*E*__, but Athlete __*A*__ ran ___*the fastest*___ of all.
   (fast)   (fast)

2. Athlete _____ ran _____. He ran _____ all the other players.
   (slow)   (slow)

3. Athlete A jumped _____ Athlete _____.
   (high)

4. Athlete _____ jumped _____ of all five athletes.
   (high)

5. Athletes B and D didn't throw the discus _____ Athlete _____.
   (far)

6. Athlete _____ threw the discus _____.
   (far)

7. Athlete _____ won in two categories. He performed _____.
   (good)

5. The Comparative of Adverbs to Express Change

Read about these athletes. Then make a statement about each. Use the correct form of the words in the box.

accurate	~~fast~~	graceful	high
far	frequent	hard	slow

1. Last month Molly ran a mile in twelve minutes. This month she's running a mile in eight minutes.

   She's running faster and faster.

2. Last month she ran three times a week. This month she's running every day.

   _____

3. Last month Billy only threw the ball ten yards. This month he's throwing it thirteen yards.

   _____

4. Last month when Jennifer shot baskets, she got only five balls in. Now when she shoots baskets,

   she gets at least eight balls in.

   _____

5. Six months ago Hank jumped only four and a half feet. Now he's jumping almost six feet.

   _____

6. Tim used to run an eight-minute mile. These days he can only run a ten-minute mile.

   _____

7. The ice-skating team of Sonia and Boris used to get four points for artistic impression. These days

   they are scoring more than five points.

   _____

8. The members of the basketball team used to practice two hours a day. Now they're practicing

   three hours a day.

   _____

6. Correct the Mistakes

Doris has been keeping an exercise journal. Read her journal entry. There are seven mistakes in the use of adverbs. Find and correct them.

4/14/94

I just completed my run. I'm running much longer than
~~that~~ before. Today I ran for thirty minutes without

getting out of breath. I'm glad I decided to run

more slow. The more slowly I run, the farthest I can

go. I'm really seeing progress. Because I'm enjoying

it, I run more and more frequent. And the more

often I do it, the longer and farther I can go. I really

believe that running lets me feel better more quick

than other forms of exercise. I'm even sleeping

better than before!

I'm thinking about running in the next marathon.

I may not run as fast than younger runners, but I

think I can run long and farther. We'll see!

U N I T

21

Gerunds: Subject and Object

▼

1. Gerund as Subject and as Object

Complete this article in a health magazine. Use the gerund form of the verbs in parentheses ( ).

KICK UP YOUR HEELS!

In recent years _____dancing_____ has become a very
　　　　　　　　　1. (dance)

popular way to stay in shape. In addition to its health

benefits, it also has social advantages. "I enjoy

_____out and _____new people," says Diana
　　2. (go)　　　　　　　　　　　3. (meet)

Romero, a 28-year-old word processor. "_____all day at a
　　　　　　　　　　　　　　　　　　　4. (sit)

computer isn't healthy. After work I need to move." And Diana isn't alone on

the dance floor. Many people who dislike _____,
　　　　　　　　　　　　　　　　　　5. (run)

_____weights, or _____sit-ups are swaying to
　　6. (lift)　　　　　　　　　　7. (do)

the beat of the swing, salsa, and rumba. So, if you are looking for an enjoyable

way to build muscles and friendships, consider _____a spin
　　　　　　　　　　　　　　　　　　　　　8. (take)

on one of the many studio dance floors that are opening up in cities across

the country. "_____ can be fun," says Sandra Carrone, owner
　　　　　9. (exercise)

of Studio Two-Step. So, quit _____time, grab a partner, and
　　　　　　　　　　　　10. (waste)

kick up your heels!

2. Gerund as Subject and as Object

Look at the results of this questionnaire on four people's likes and dislikes.
Then complete the sentences below with appropriate gerunds.

Key: + = enjoy
      √ = don't mind
      − = dislike

	DIANA	HECTOR	MINH	AMY
1. dance	+	−	+	−
2. walk	+	+	+	+
3. do situps	−	+	−	−
4. play tennis	−	√	+	−
5. jog	−	+	√	−
6. lift weights	√	√	−	+

1. Hector is the only one who enjoys _____*doing situps*_____.

2. Minh doesn't like _____, but Diana doesn't mind it.

3. Diana enjoys _____, but Amy really dislikes it.

4. _____ is the activity that people most disliked.

5. Half of the people don't mind _____.

6. _____ is an activity that half of the people enjoy.

7. _____ is the only activity that all four enjoy.

8. Diana and Minh are going to go _____ together at the Two-Step Studio.

   They both enjoy it.

9. Amy and Diana dislike _____.

10. They also dislike _____.

3. Gerund after Certain Verbs

Sandra Carrone is having a dance party at her studio. Complete the conversations.
Complete the summary sentences with the appropriate verbs from the box and use the
gerund form of the verbs in parentheses ( ).

admit	deny	enjoy	~~mind~~ ~~quit~~	regret
consider	dislike	keep		suggest

1. **Minh:** Would you like a cup of coffee?

   Diana: No, thanks. I haven't had coffee in five years.

   Diana _____*quit drinking*_____ coffee five years ago.
   (drink)

2. **Oscar:** Oh, they're playing a tango. Would you like to dance?

   Rika: No, thanks. It's not my favorite dance.

   Rika _____ the tango.
   (do)

3. **Amy:** Do you often come to these dance parties?

   Barbara: Yes. It's a good opportunity to dance with a lot of different partners.

   Barbara _____ with different partners.
   (dance)

4. **Laura:** I don't know how to do the cha-cha. Could you show me?

   Bill: OK. Just follow me.

   Bill doesn't _____ Laura the cha-cha.
   (teach)

5. **Diana:** This is a difficult dance. How did you learn it?

   Minh: I practiced it again and again.

   Minh _____ the dance.
   (practice)

6. **Vera:** Ow. You stepped on my toe!

   Luis: No, I didn't!

   Luis _____ on Vera's toe.
   (step)

7. **Bill:** Are you going to take any more classes?

   Laura: I'm not sure. I haven't decided yet. Maybe.

   Laura is _____ more dance classes.
   (take)

(Continued on next page.)

8. **Diana:** I really love dancing.

   Minh: Me too. I'm sorry I didn't start years ago. It's a lot of fun.

   Minh _____ dance lessons sooner.
   (not begin)

9. **Bill:** Why don't we go out for coffee after class next week?

   Laura: OK. I'd like that.

   Bill _____ out after class.
   (go)

10. **Minh:** You look tired.

    Laura: I *am* tired. I think this will be the last dance for me.

    Laura _____ tired.
    (feel)

1. Prepositions after Certain Verbs and Adjectives

Complete the chart with the correct preposition. You will use some prepositions more than once.

about	for	in	of	on	to

1. look forward ___*to*___

2. be tired _____

3. be used _____

4. insist _____

5. believe _____

6. apologize _____

7. approve _____

8. succeed _____

9. be worried _____

10. be opposed _____

2. Gerunds after Prepositions

Read these conversations that take place at a student council meeting. Rewrite them. Use the expressions in Exercise 1 and the gerund form of the verbs in parentheses ( ).

1. **Allen:** Where were you? It's 7:30. Our meeting started at 7:00.

   Bob: I know. I'm sorry.

   Bob _____*apologized for coming*_____ late.

                             (come)

2. **Mark:** I have some good news to report. We've reached our goal. Since

   our last meeting, we've collected more than 100 student

   signatures in favor of going on strike.

   The students _____(collect)_____ more than

   100 signatures.

(Continued on next page.)

3. **Amy:** I'm not so sure it's a good idea to strike.

   Bob: Final exams are in a few weeks. It'll be a problem if we miss classes.

Bob _____ classes.
(miss)

4. **Amy:** I don't know. We've always solved our problems with the administration before.

   Bob: That's true. In the past they've always listened to us.

These students _____ with the administration to solve
(work)
their problems.

5. **Amy:** I don't think we should go on strike. I think we should talk to the administration again.

   Bob: I agree. That's the best way to solve this problem.

Amy and Bob _____ to the administration again.
(talk)

6. **Mark:** We've been asking the administration for a response for weeks. They've said nothing.

   Eva: That's right. We've had enough. We don't want to wait any more.

These students _____ for an answer.
(wait)

7. **Bob:** Can we give this decision a little more time?

   Mark: No, I'm sorry. We really *have to* reach a decision today.

Mark _____ a decision immediately.
(reach)

8. **Mark:** Let's take a vote. All those in favor of going on strike raise your hand....OK. That's 10 for

   and 2 against. That means we recommend a strike to the student body.

The student council _____ a strike.
(have)

9. **Mark:** Well, that's settled.

   Eva: Only two people voted no.

Only two council members _____ on strike.
(go)

10. **Amy:** I don't know about you, but I'll be glad when all this is over.

    Bob: I know what you mean. I'll be happy when things return to normal.

Amy and Bob are _____ to their normal activities.
(return)

3. Gerunds after Prepositions

Complete this editorial in the student newspaper. Use the gerund form of the appropriate verbs from the box.

be	get	hear	miss	strike
fire	~~get~~	make	permit	try

Yesterday the student council voted 10 to 2 in favor of _____going_____ on strike. By
1.
_____ they hope to reverse the
2.
administration's decision to fire two popular

teachers. The students are against

_____ teachers because of their
3.
political views. They believe in

_____ the free expression of all
4.
opinions. They feel that teachers, as well as

students, should be able to say what they want

without _____ afraid of the
5.
administration's reaction.

   If the student council succeeds in

_____ student support, the
6.

strike will begin on Tuesday. Not all students,

however, support the idea of a strike. Many are

afraid of _____ classes just a
7.
few weeks before exam time. They haven't

given up _____ to solve the
8.
problem with the administration. Other students

haven't made up their minds yet. Which side

are you on? Before _____ a
9.
final decision, we suggest that you attend the

students' meeting on Monday at 4:00. After

_____ both sides, it may be
10.
easier to make a decision.

1. Infinitives after Certain Verbs

Read this exchange of letters in an advice column. Use the cues to complete the letters. Choose the correct tense of the first verb and use the infinitive form of the second verb.

Dear Gabby,

I've known John for two years. Last month we ___*decided to get*___ married. Since then
1. (decide/get)
our relationship has been a nightmare. John

criticizes me for every little thing, and we are

constantly fighting. I _____ a
2. (want/see)
marriage counselor, but John

_____ with me. Last night he
3. (refuse/go)
even _____ the relationship if I
4. (threaten/end)
mention the idea of counseling again.

I don't understand what's going on. We used

to get along great. I still love John, but I

_____ the next step.
5. (hesitate/take)
What should I do?

One Step Out the Door

Dear One Step Out the Door,

I've heard your story many times before.

John _____ afraid of getting
6. (seem/be)
married. As soon as you got engaged, he

_____ distance by fighting
7. (attempt/create)
with you. I agree that counseling is a good idea

if you _____ together. Maybe
8. (intend/stay)
each of you _____ to a
9. (need/speak)
counselor separately before going to one

together. It's possible that John

_____ alone to discuss some of
10. (agree/go)
his fears.

Gabby

2. Verb + Infinitive or Verb + Object + Infinitive

Read some typical conversations that take place between men and women in relationships. Complete the summary statements.

1. **She:** I *really* think you should see a therapist.

   He: I'm not going to.

   She urged *him to see a therapist.* _____

   He refused *to see a therapist.* _____

2. **He:** You do the dishes.

   She: No, you do the dishes.

   He didn't want _____

   She wanted _____

3. **He:** Don't forget to buy some milk.

   She: OK. I'll get some on the way home.

   He reminded _____

   She agreed _____

4. **She:** Will you do me a favor? Could you drive me to my aunt's?

   He: OK.

   She asked _____

   He agreed _____

5. **She:** Would you like to have dinner at my place Friday night?

   He: Uhm. I'm not sure. Uhm. I guess so.

   She invited _____

   He hesitated _____

6. **She:** Will you give me your answer tomorrow?

   He: Yes, I will. That's a promise.

   She wants _____

   He promised _____

(Continued on next page.)

7. **She:** Would you like me to cut your hair? It's really long.

   He: Oh, OK.

   She offered _____

   He is going to allow _____

8. **She:** It's 8:00. I thought you said you'd be home at 7:00.

   He: No. I always get home at 8:00.

   She expected _____

   He expected _____

1. Affirmative and Negative Statements

Read the pairs of sentences. Combine them, using the infinitive of purpose.

1. I went to Lacy's department store. I wanted to buy some clothes.

   I went to Lacy's department store to buy some clothes.

2. He bought an alarm clock. He didn't want to oversleep.

   He bought an alarm clock in order not to oversleep.

3. She used her credit card. She didn't want to pay right away.

   _____

4. I asked for the dressing room. I wanted to try on a dress.

   _____

5. They went to the snack bar. They wanted to get a drink.

   _____

6. I'm going to wait for a sale. I want to save some money.

   _____

7. She tried on the blouse. She wanted to be sure of the size.

   _____

8. He only took fifty dollars with him. He didn't want to spend more.

   _____

9. They went to Lacy's on Monday. They didn't want to miss the sale.

   _____

10. She asked the salesclerk to show her the scarf. She wanted to feel the

    material.

    _____

2. Affirmative and Negative Statements

These conversations take place in a department store. Complete them. Use the verbs in the box and the infinitive of purpose.

~~ask~~	cut	have	pay	sign
carry	find out	miss	return	waste

1. **A:** Before we start looking around, I want to go to the information desk.

   B: Oh. Why do you need to go there?

   A: _____ *To ask* _____ where the petites department is. I can never find it. They keep changing

   its location.

2. **A:** I'd like to return this.

   B: Do you have the receipt?

   A: No, I don't. I got it as a gift, and I really can't use it.

   B: Hmm. I see there's no price tag on it. I'm sorry, but you need the receipt or the price tag

   _____ it.

3. **A:** Do you always pay by credit card?

   B: Most of the time. What about you?

   A: No. I don't like to pay finance charges. It ends up being more expensive that way.

   B: I know what you mean. I always try to pay the bill immediately _____ a finance

   charge.

4. **A:** Can I please have a shopping bag?

   B: Sure.

   A: Thanks. I need one _____ all this stuff.

5. **A:** Do you have a pen?

   B: Here you are.

   A: Thanks. I need one _____ my name.

6. **A:** I'm hungry.

   B: Me too. Let's go to the food court _____ a snack.

   A: Good idea. I always get hungry when I go shopping.

7. **A:** Excuse me. Do you have a sharper knife? I need one _____ this steak. It's a little

   tough.

   B: I'm sorry. I'll bring you one right away.

8. **A:** How do those shoes fit?

   B: I'm not sure. They may be a little tight.

   A: Walk around a little _____ if they're the right size.

9. **A:** We should leave now.

   B: Why? It's only 5:00.

   A: I know. But we have to leave now _____ the express bus.

10. **A:** Here's the up escalator, but where's the escalator going down?

    B: Oh, let's just take the elevator _____ time.

25

Infinitives with Too and Enough

▼

1. Word Order

Put the words in the correct order to make sentences about a new job.

A: Tell me about your new job.

B: Well, like most jobs it has its positive and negative points.

1. near/for me/it's/to walk to work/enough

   It's near enough for me to walk to work.   +

2. too/It's/noisy/for me/to concentrate

   _____

3. varied/to be interesting/the work/enough/is

   _____

4. for me/the salary/enough/to support my family/is/high

   _____

5. to hold/my desk/small/is/too/all my things

   _____

6. late/I/sleep/enough/can/to feel awake in the morning

   _____

7. for me/my boss/quickly/to understand him/speaks/too

   _____

8. aren't/low/the bookshelves/to reach/for me/enough

   _____

Now look at the sentences you wrote. Put a plus (+) next to all the positive points. Put a minus (–) next to all the negative points.

| **2.** | Infinitives with *Too* and *Enough* |

Complete these conversations that take place at the workplace.

1. **A:** Can you read the boss's handwriting?

   B: No. It's ___*too messy for me to read*___.
   (messy/me/read)

2. **A:** It's 11:00 A.M. Do you think we can call Mr. Lin in San Francisco?

   B: Sure. It's 8:00 A.M. there. That's _____.
   (late/call)

3. **A:** Could you help me with those boxes?

   B: Sorry. They're _____. I have a bad back.
   (heavy/me/carry)

4. **A:** This coffee is terrible.

   B: What's the matter with it?

   A: It's_____. It tastes like someone put
   (sweet/drink)
   about four tablespoons of sugar in it.

5. **A:** Do you think we can put the fax machine on that shelf?

   B: Sure. It's _____.
   (small/fit)

6. **A:** Hey, guys. Can you keep the noise down, please? It's _____.
   (noisy/me/think)

   B: Sorry. We'll try to be quieter.

7. **A:** Did you hear that Alex is retiring?

   B: You're kidding! He's not even fifty. He's _____.
   (old/retire)

8. **A:** Can you turn on the air conditioner, please?

   B: The air conditioner! It's _____ the air conditioner.
   (hot/need)
   What are you going to do in August when it really gets hot?

9. **A:** I don't feel well. I think I'm going to go home early.

   B: Maybe you should call the doctor.

   A: Oh. I'm _____ the doctor. I just need to get some rest.
   (sick/call)

10. **A:** Can you help me get that box?

    B: Sure.

    A: Thanks. It's_____.
    (high/me/reach)

3. Correct the Mistakes

Read this letter home from a teenager in Boy Scout camp. He made six mistakes in the use of the infinitive with **too** *and* **enough**. *Find and correct them.*

Dear Mom and Dad,

      too

I'm almost ~~to~~ tired to write. I can't believe how hard Boy Scout camp is. Today we went out on a two-hour hike. It was over 90° in the shade! It was too hot for to think. We had to take a lot of stuff with us, too. My backpack was too heavy for me to lift it. I don't think I'm too strong to complete the program. How did I get into this mess? Is it too late too get out? Please write.

              Love,

              Tommy

P.S. The food is terrible. It's not enough good to eat. Can you send some candy bars?

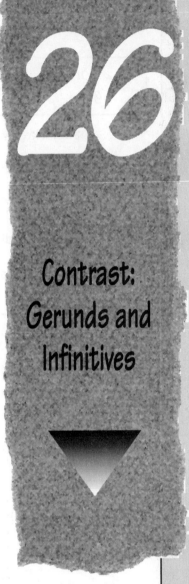

1. Gerund or Infinitive

Complete this notice about neighborhood crime prevention. Use the correct form of the verbs in parentheses ( ).

Join Your Neighborhood Watch 🏠

_____*Making*_____ our neighborhood safe is our main concern.
1. (make)
Here are some safety tips:

* Remember ____*to lock*____ your doors and windows
  2. (lock)
  when you go out.

* Don't forget _____ some lights on when
  3. (leave)
  you're not at home.

* Avoid _____ alone on dark, deserted streets.
  4. (walk)

* Learn _____ aware of your surroundings.
  5. (be)

* Don't stop _____ for your house keys.
  6. (look)
  Have them in your hand before you get to the door.

* Consider _____ a class in self-defense.
  7. (take)
  The Adult Center offers free classes.

* Don't hesitate _____ a police officer for help.
  8. (ask)
  It's better to be safe than sorry.

Stop _____ in fear. Join your Neighborhood Watch.
9. (live)
The next meeting is on Tuesday, March 3, at the Community Center,

7:00 P.M.

Please attend! We look forward to _____ you there!
10. (see)

2. Gerund or Infinitive

These conversations took place at a community center. Complete the summary statements about them. Choose the right verbs or expressions from the box and use the gerund or infinitive form of the verbs in parentheses ( ).

afford	be tired of	~~enjoy~~	intend	quit	remember
agree	believe in	forget	offer	refuse	stop

1. **Joe:** Have you ever been to one of these meetings before?

   Nancy: Yes. You get a lot of useful tips. Besides, I like to meet my neighbors.

   Nancy _____*enjoys meeting*_____ her neighbors.
   (meet)

2. **Andrea:** Why did you start coming to these meetings?

   Frank: My apartment was broken into twice. I've had enough. I want to do something about it.

   Frank _____ a crime victim.
   (be)

3. **Craig:** Would you like a cup of coffee?

   Sylvie: Oh, no thanks.

   Craig: Don't you drink coffee?

   Sylvie: I used to, but I gave it up a year ago.

   Sylvie _____ coffee.
   (drink)

4. **Caryn:** I think these meetings are really important. You can get a lot accomplished when you

   work with other people.

   Fernando: I know what you mean.

   Caryn _____ with other people.
   (work)

5. **Jane:** Did you bring Gerry's book?

   Sara: Oh, no. I left it at work.

   Jane _____ Gerry's book.
   (bring)

6. **Sharon:** Did you lock the windows before we left the house?

   Jim: No, *you* locked the windows. I saw you do it.

   Sharon: That's strange. I don't _____ them!
   (lock)

7. **Tom:** You're late. I was getting worried.

    Betsy: I'm sorry. On the way over here, I noticed that I was almost out of gas. So I went to fill

    up the tank.

    Betsy _____ gas.
    _____(get)_____

8. **Cathy:** I really don't like the neighborhood anymore.

    Mike: So why don't you move?

    Cathy: The rents are too high everywhere else.

    Cathy can't _____.
    _____(move)_____

9. **Camille:** I was afraid to come to the meeting tonight.

    Vilma: Well, I just *won't* live in fear.

    Vilma _____ in fear.
    _____(live)_____

10. **Sara:** Do you have a burglar alarm?

    Dave: No. But I'm definitely going to get one.

    Dave _____ a burglar alarm.
    _____(get)_____

11. **Rachel:** Do you think you could help us organize the next meeting?

    Walter: OK.

    Walter _____ with the next meeting.
    _____(help)_____

12. **Axel:** Would you like a ride home?

    Joanna: Thanks. That would be great.

    Axel _____ Joanna home.
    _____(drive)_____

3. Gerund or Infinitive

Rewrite these sentences. Use the gerund or infinitive.

1. It's important to know your neighbors.

   Knowing your neighbors is important.

2. Going to the community center is fun.

   It's fun to go to the community center.

3. It's wise to be cautious.

   _____

4. Walking on ice is dangerous.

   _____

5. Installing a burglar alarm is a good idea.

   _____

6. It's not good to be afraid all the time.

   _____

7. Walking alone on a dark, deserted street is risky.

   _____

8. Working together is helpful.

   _____

U N I T

27

1. Affirmative and Negative Statements with *Can* and *Could*

Read about this student's ability in English. Make statements.

Ability: Can, Could, Be able to ▼

Student's Name ___Fernando Ochoa___

English Language Ability Questionnaire

SKILL	NOW	BEFORE THIS COURSE
1. understand conversational English	√	✗
2. understand recorded announcements	✗	✗
3. read an English newspaper	√	√
4. read an English novel	✗	✗
5. speak on the phone	√	✗
6. speak with a group of people	√	✗
7. write a social letter	√	✗
8. write a business letter	✗	✗
9. order a meal in English	√	√
10. go shopping	√	√

1. Before this course he ___couldn't understand conversational English.___
   Now ___he can understand conversational English.___

2. He___couldn't understand recorded announcements___ before the course,
   and he still ___can't understand them.___

3. He _____ now, and he
   _____ before, too.

4. He _____ before the course, and he still
   _____

5. Now he _____, but before the course he
   _____

6. Before the course, he _____,
   but now he _____

(Continued on next page.)

7. Before the course, he_____.

   Now he _____

8. _____

   _____

9. _____

   _____

10. _____

    _____

Summary: Fernando _____ do a lot more now than he

_____ before the course.

2. Questions and Answers with Can and Could

Complete this interview with another student.

1. **A:** (speak/any other languages?)

   *Can you speak any other languages?*_____

   B: _____ *Yes, I can.* _____ I speak two other languages.

2. **A:** (What/languages/speak?)

   _____

   B: Spanish and French.

3. **A:** (speak Spanish/when you were a child?)

   _____

   B: _____ I learned it as an adult.

4. **A:** (speak French?)

   _____

   B: _____ We spoke French some of the time at home.

5. **A:** (Before you came here/understand spoken English?)

   _____

   B: _____ I didn't understand anything!

6. **A:** What about now? (understand song lyrics?)

   _____

   B: _____ Especially if I listen to them more than once.

7. **A:** (Before this course/write a business letter in English?)

   _____

   B: _____ But I used to write in English to my friends.

8. **A:** Enough about languages. Tell me some more about yourself. For example, (drive a car before you came here?)

   _____

   B: _____ I was too young.

9. **A:** (drive a car now?)

   _____

   B: _____ I still haven't learned.

10. **A:** (What/do now/that/not do before?)

    _____

    B: Oh! I _____ a lot of things now that I _____ before.

| **3.** | Affirmative and Negative Statements with *Be able to* |

Complete this article about hearing loss. Use the correct form of **be able to**
and the verbs in parentheses ( ).

There are more than 26 million people in the United States who have some degree of hearing loss. There are two major types of hearing loss.

1. **Sound Sensitivity Loss.** People with this kind of loss ___*are not able to hear*___ soft
   $\quad\quad\quad\quad\quad\quad\quad\quad\quad\quad\quad\quad\quad$ 1. (not hear)

   sounds—a whisper or a bird singing, for example. However, when sounds are loud enough,

   they _____ them correctly.
   $\quad\quad\quad$ 2. (interpret)

(Continued on next page.)

2. **Sound Discrimination Loss.** People with this kind of hearing loss

_____ one sound from another. As a result of this, they
     3. (not distinguish)

_____ speech—even when it is loud enough for them to hear.
     4. (not understand)

How do people with hearing disabilities cope in a hearing world? Most people with hearing

impairments _____ some sounds. Since the widespread availability of the
     5. (hear)

hearing aid, many people _____ some of their ability to hear. Some people
     6. (regain)

with hearing disabilities _____ lips. But, at best, lip reading is only 30 to
     7. (read)

50 percent effective. Even a good lip-reader _____ all the sounds. Just ask
     8. (not recognize)

someone to silently mouth the words *pat, bat,* and *mat.* They sound different, but they all *look*

the same. Besides, the human eye _____ fast enough to process speech
     9. (not work)

by vision alone. By far, the most successful form of communication is signing—the use of sign

language. People with hearing impairments _____ successfully with
     10. (communicate)

others who know this language.

4.   Questions and Short Answers with *Be Able to*

*Sensitivity to sound is measured in decibels. Look at this chart. It shows the
decibel measurements of some common sounds.*

0 decibels	softest sound a typical ear can hear
20 decibels	a whisper
45 decibels	soft conversational speech
55 decibels	loud conversational speech
65 decibels	loud music from the radio
75 decibels	city traffic
100 decibels	loud factory noise
110 decibels	loud amplified rock band
120 decibels	loud power tool
140 decibels	jet engine at takeoff

Source: Rezen and Hausman, *Coping with Hearing Loss: A Guide for Adults
and their Families,* New York: Dembner Books, 1985.

Mary has a hearing loss of 50 decibels. This means she will not be able to hear sounds that have a loudness of 50 decibels or less. Ask and answer these questions about what Mary will be able to hear at the party she is going to.

1. **A:** _Will she be able to hear_ _____ a whisper?

   B: _No, she won't._ _____

2. **A:** _____ loud music?

   B: _____

3. **A:** _____ a soft conversation?

   B: _____

4. **A:** _____ loud traffic?

   B: _____

5. **A:** _____ a loud conversation?

   B: _____

5. Contrast: Can and *Be Able to*

Read this information about a well-known actress who is deaf. Complete it with the correct form of **can** *or* **be able to** *and the verbs in parentheses ( ). Use* **can** *or* **could** *when possible.*

Actress Marlee Matlin ____ *could hear* ____ at birth but lost her hearing at the age of 18 months as a
      1. (hear)

result of a childhood illness. By the age of five, she _____ lips. Shortly after that, she
                                                   2. (read)

mastered sign language. At first, Matlin felt angry and frightened by her hearing impairment. "I wanted

to be perfect, and I _____ my deafness," she said during an interview. With time, howev-
                    3. (not accept)

er, she _____ to accept it.
        4. (learn)

Matlin began her acting career at the age of eight, when she performed in theater for the deaf. In

1986, she received an Oscar nomination for best actress in the Hollywood film, *Children of a Lesser*

God. In the movie she played the role of an angry woman who was deaf and did not want to speak. For

(Continued on next page.)

Matlin, however, speaking is very important. At the Oscar ceremonies, she _____ her

5. (accept)

award verbally. It was the first time the public heard her speak. "It's what I wanted to do, because a lot

of people all over the world _____ me for who I am," she said. Matlin was worried, how-

6. (see)

ever. "What other roles _____ I _____ in the future?" she asked.

7. (do)

Since her Oscar award, Matlin has appeared in another Hollywood movie, a television movie, and

has co-starred in her own TV series, *Reasonable Doubts*. One reviewer said about Matlin, "She

_____ more saying nothing than most people _____ talking."

8. (do)   9. (do)

Matlin doesn't think of herself as a "deaf actress." She is an "actress who happens to be deaf." She

_____ both the deaf and hearing worlds. Since recent intensive speech training, she

10. (master)

_____ very clearly, and in the future, she hopes she _____ roles that are

11. (speak)   12. (get)

not specifically written for people with hearing impairments.

---

6. Find the Mistakes

Read this student's composition. There are seven mistakes in the use of **can**
and **be able to***. Find and correct them.*

> couldn't
> Before I came to this country I ~~can't~~ do many things in English.
> For example, I couldn't follow a conversation if many people
> were talking at the same time. I remember one occasion at a
> party. I wasn't able understand a word! I felt so uncomfortable.
> Finally, my aunt came to pick me up, and I could leave the party.
>
> Today I can to understand much better. Since last month I can
> practice a lot. I am taking classes at the adult center. My teacher
> is very good. She can explains things well, and she always gives
> us the chance to talk a lot in class. I can do a lot now, and I think
> in a few more months I can do even more.

7. Personalization

Look at the English Language Ability Questionnaire in Exercise 1. Write sentences about your English ability now and before this course.

1. _____

   _____

2. _____

   _____

3. _____

   _____

4. _____

   _____

28

Permission: May, Could, Can, Do you mind if...?

1. Questions and Responses

Match these classroom questions and responses.

QUESTIONS

1. __*d*__ Do you mind if I bring some friends to class?

2. _____ May I ask a question?

3. _____ Do you mind if I tape the lesson?

4. _____ Could I open the window?

5. _____ Can we review Unit 4?

6. _____ May I leave the room?

7. _____ Could we use our dictionaries?

8. _____ Could I borrow a pen?

RESPONSES

a. Certainly. The key to the rest room is hanging on the wall.

b. Not at all.

c. Sure. I hope I can answer it.

d. Actually, I do mind. It's already pretty crowded.

e. Sure. But remember, you don't have to look up every word.

f. I'm afraid we can't. We're running out of time.

g. Sure. But please remember to return it.

h. Go right ahead. It's quite warm in here.

2. Questions

Read the situations. Complete the questions.

1. You want to open the window.

   May __*I open the window?*__

2. Your whole class wants to review Unit 6.

   Could _____

3. You want to borrow a classmate's pen.

   Can _____

4. You want to look at someone's class notes.

   Do you mind if _____

5. You want to come late to the next class.

   Do you mind if _____

6. Your husband wants to come to the next class with you.

   Could _____

7. You want to ask a question.

   May _____

8. You and a classmate would like to use a dictionary.

   Can _____

9. You and your classmates want to leave five minutes early.

   Could _____

10. Your sister wants to go on the class trip with the rest of the class.

   Do you mind if _____

3. Affirmative and Negative Statements

Look at the flier. Complete the statements. Use the words in parentheses ( ).

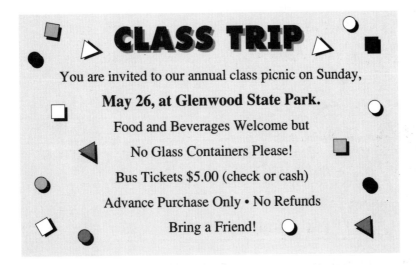

CLASS TRIP

You are invited to our annual class picnic on Sunday,

May 26, at Glenwood State Park.

Food and Beverages Welcome but

No Glass Containers Please!

Bus Tickets $5.00 (check or cash)

Advance Purchase Only • No Refunds

Bring a Friend!

1. You _____*may bring*_____ a friend.
      (may/bring)

2. You _____ your own food.
      (can/bring)

3. You _____ juice from a glass bottle at the picnic.
      (can/drink)

4. You _____ for your bus ticket by check.
      (can/pay)

(Continued on next page.)

5. You _____ for your bus ticket by cash.
(can/pay)

6. You _____ for your ticket by credit card.
(may/pay)

7. You _____ your bus ticket on the day of the trip.
(may/purchase)

8. You _____ a refund.
(can/get)

4. Personalization

*Imagine that you are in class. Read the following situations. Ask your
teacher for permission to do something.*

1. You don't understand something the teacher is saying.

_____

2. You don't feel well.

_____

3. Your cousin from (your country) is going to visit you for a week.

_____

1. Requests and Responses

Match these office requests and responses.

REQUESTS

1. __*d*__ Could you meet me tomorrow morning at 8:00?

2. _____ Will you please type this memo for me?

3. _____ Would you please spell your last name for me?

4. _____ Would you mind taking this letter to the post office?

5. _____ Can you cancel tomorrow's meeting for me? I have to go out of town.

6. _____ Will you shut the window, please?

7. _____ Would you get that box of computer paper from the closet?

8. _____ Could you get the phone for me?

RESPONSES

a. I'd be glad to. When do you need it?

b. Sure. It is pretty cold in here.

c. Of course, I can. When would you like to reschedule it?

d. I'm sorry. I have an early morning dentist appointment.

e. Sure...."Hello, J and R Equities."

f. Sure. It's M-A-R-D-J-A-I-T.

g. I'd like to, but it's too heavy for me to lift.

h. Not at all.

Requests: Will, Would, Could, Can, Would you mind...?

Write the numbers of the requests that were granted: ___*2,*_____

Write the numbers of the requests that were refused: _____

113

2. Requests

These conversations take place in an office. Complete them, using the phrases in the box.

~~answer the phone~~	lend me $5.00
come to my office	mail a letter
explain this note to me	open the window
get Frank's phone number	pick up a sandwich
keep the noise down	stay late tonight

1. **A:** Could you _answer the phone?_ _____

   My hands are full

   B: Sure. I'll get it.

2. **A:** Would you mind _____

   It's really hot in here.

   B: No, not at all.

3. **A:** Can you please _____ for me?

   B: Certainly. I pass the post office on my way home.

4. **A:** I'm going to the coffee shop. Can I get you anything?

   B: Could you _____ for me?

   A: Sure.

5. **A:** Would you mind _____

   I really have to get this report done by tomorrow.

   B: I'm sorry, but I have to visit my aunt in the hospital.

6. **A:** Will you _____ please?

   I can't hear myself think!

   B: Sorry!

7. **A:** Can you _____ when you have the chance?

   B: Sure. I'll be right there.

8. **A:** Would you _____ for me?

   B: It's 555-4345.

9. **A:** Would you mind _____

   B: Not at all. What is it that you don't understand?

10. **A:** Could you _____

    B: Oh, I'm sorry. I'm short on cash.

3. Find the Mistakes

There are four mistakes in these office notes. Find and correct them.

1.

> Meng,
> Would you ~~filed~~ file these,
> please?
> Thanks.
>   R.L.

2.

> Hi Ted,
>   Could you please
> remember to turn off the
> lights when you leave?
>   Thanks,
>   Lynn

3.

> Hank,
> Will you return please the stapler?
>   Brad

4.

> Melida,
> Can you make 5 copies
> of these pages, please?
> Thanks.
>   Ellen

(Continued on next page.)

5.

John,
Would you mind
leave the finished
report on my desk?
Roy

6.

Celia,
Could you please remember
to lock the door.
Thank you.
Diana

4. Personalization

Write one request that you would like to make of each of the following people.

1. (To your teacher) _____

2. (To a classmate) _____

3. (To your boss) _____

4. (To your landlord) _____

5. (To _____) _____

1. Questions and Answers with Should

Read this invitation. Use the information in the invitation to complete the phone conversation.

YOU ARE INVITED TO A PARTY!

FOR: _Scott's SURPRISE graduation barbecue_

DATE: _June 11_

TIME: _2:00 P.M. sharp!_

PLACE: _20 Greenport Avenue_

RSVP by May 15. Please don't call here!
Leave a message at 555-3234.
            No Gifts, Please
(but please bring something to drink)

Wanda: Hi, Tania.

Tania: Hi, Wanda. What's up?

Wanda: Aunt Rosa's having a graduation party for Scott. She didn't have

your new address, so she asked me to call and invite you. It's on

June 11. Can you come?

Tania: Sure. Just give me all the information. (What time/be there?)

What time should I be there?
                                    1.

Wanda: Let's see. I have the invitation right here.

You should be there at 2:00 P.M. sharp.
                                    2.

Tania: (What/wear?)

_____
                                    3.

Wanda: Something casual. It's a barbecue.

Tania: (bring a gift?)

_____
                                    4.

(Continued on next page.)

Wanda: _____ The invitation says "no gifts."
5.

Tania: OK. What about food? (bring something to eat or drink?)

_____
6.

Wanda: _____
7.

Oh, and the invitation says "RSVP." In other words, Aunt Rosa wants a response.

Tania: (When/I respond?)

_____
8.

Wanda: _____
9.

Tania: (call Aunt Rosa?)

_____
10.

Wanda: _____ I forgot to tell you. It's a surprise party!
11.

Tania: OK. (Who/call?)

_____
12.

Wanda: _____
13.

Tania: Fine. Sounds like fun. I'll see you there. Thanks for calling.

Wanda: No problem. See you there.

2. Affirmative and Negative Statements with *Had better*

Friends are giving Scott advice about looking for a job. Complete the advice.
*Use **had better** or **had better not** and the appropriate verbs from the box.*

| arrive | dress | have | ~~look at~~ | thank |
| ask | go | leave | chew | write |

1. _You'd better look at_ the newspaper want ads every day.

2. _____ your old job before you find a new one. That way you'll always have

some money coming in.

3. _____ late for a job interview.

4. _____ a good resume.

5. _____ nicely when you go on an interview. Don't wear your jeans!

6. _____ gum during an interview.

7. _____ for too much money right away. You can always get a raise after

you begin.

8. _____ the interviewer at the end of the interview.

9. _____ on a lot of interviews. It's good practice.

10. _____ a lot of patience. It can take a long time.

3. **Questions and Answers: *Should, Ought to, and Had better***

Scott is getting ready for a job interview. Complete his conversation with a friend. Use **should, ought to,** *and* **had better.** *Sometimes more than one answer is possible.*

Scott: _____*Should I wear*_____ my green suit?
                    1. (wear)

Dennis: I don't think so. I think _____ your navy blue one. It's more
                                          2. (wear)

conservative.

Scott: _____ my boss about the interview?
                    3. (tell)

Dennis: No. _____ until you get a job before you say anything to your old
                      4. (wait)

boss.

Scott: I think we're going out for lunch after the interview. _____ to pay?
                                                                        5. (offer)

Dennis: I don't think so. _____ for your lunch. The interviewer usually
                                6. (pay)

does that.

Scott: _____ a thank-you note after the interview?
                    7. (write)

Dennis: That's always a good idea.

Scott: When _____ it?
                      8. (send)

Dennis: _____ a few days. That way you can always include something you
                  9. (wait)

forgot to say during the interview.

Scott: Well, _____ to say anything important!
                      10. (not forget)

Dennis: Try to relax. I'm sure you'll do fine.

Scott: I hope so. _____ you after the interview?
                            11. (call)

Dennis: _____ me or I'll never speak to you again!
                  12. (call)

4. Personalization

A friend of yours is very unhappy at his or her job. Give your friend some advice.

1. _____

2. _____

3. _____

4. _____

5. _____

1. Suggestions

Match the two halves of each suggestion. Notice the end punctuation—period (.)
or question mark (?).

1. _c_ My feet hurt. Why don't we

2. ____ The weather's terrible.
    How about

3. ____ We have an hour before the
    show starts. We could

4. ____ You look exhausted. Why
    don't I

5. ____ This concert is terrible.
    Let's not

6. ____ I'm really hungry. How about

7. ____ There's so much to see!
    How about

8. ____ If John's unhappy at the Blue
    Water Inn, why doesn't he

9. ____ It's going to be hot
    tomorrow. Let's

10. ____ There's a gift shop.
    Maybe we could

a. going to a movie?

b. have a cup of coffee.

c. take a taxi?

d. go to the beach.

e. getting a slice of pizza?

f. change hotels?

g. meet you back at the hotel?

h. buy some
    souvenirs there.

i. taking a walking tour?

j. stay until the end.

Suggestions:
Let's,
How about...?,
Why don't...?,
Why not...?

2. Punctuation

Circle the correct phrase in italics to complete these conversations between tourists on vacation. Add the correct punctuation—period (.) or question mark (?).

1. **A:** I'm exhausted. We've been walking for hours.

   B: *How about/(Why don't we)* sit on that bench for a while ____?___

2. **A:** I'm almost out of film.

   B: There's a drugstore over there. *Maybe you could/Let's not* get film there _____

3. **A:** It would be nice to see some of the countryside.

   B: *Let's/How about* rent a car _____

4. **A:** *Why not/How about* taking a bus tour _____

   B: That's a good idea. It's less expensive than renting a car.

5. **A:** I want to take a picture of that building. *Why don't you/How about* stand in front of it _____

   B: OK.

6. **A:** We have an hour before we have to meet the rest of our tour group.

   B: *Let's/Let's not* get a cup of coffee in that cafe _____

   A: Good idea. I could use something to drink.

7. **A:** I heard it's going to rain tomorrow.

   B: *Maybe we could/How about* go to a museum _____

8. **A:** I really need to get a better map of the city.

   B: *Why don't you/Let's not* stop at that tourist information office _____ I'm sure they

   have maps.

9. **A:** I don't know what to get for my daughter.

   B: *Why don't you/How about* getting one of those sweatshirts _____

10. **A:** Look at that beautiful building. Why don't you take a picture of it?

    B: *That's a good idea/Because I don't want to* _____

3. Suggestions

Look at the tourist information. Complete the conversation. Use the suggestions in the pamphlet.

BOSTON Highlights

Here are some of the many things you can do in this "capital of New England"

☆ **Go to Haymarket**—open-air fruit and vegetable stands (Fridays and Saturdays only) ☆

✓ ☆ **Visit Faneuil Hall Market Place** —restoration of Boston's historic Quincy Market. Shops, restaurants ☆

☆ **Go to The New England Aquarium**—412 species, 7,606 specimens ☆

☆ **Walk along the waterfront**—offices, shops, parks for picnics ☆

☆ **Take the "T"**—Boston's subway system ☆

☆ **Take a boat excursion**—cruise the harbor and Massachusetts Bay ($1^1/2$ hours) ☆

☆ **Go shopping in Downtown Crossing**—Boston's pedestrian zone ☆

☆ **Take an elevator to the top of the John Hancock Observatory**—the tallest building in New England ☆

☆ **Walk the Freedom Trail**—$1^1/2$ miles of historic points of interest ☆

☆ **Eat at Legal Seafoods**—restaurant chain famous for fresh fish at reasonable prices. (No reservations accepted) ☆

A: Wow, there's so much to do! I don't know where to begin!

B: Why don't we ___*visit Faneuil Hall Market Place*___? We can have breakfast there and then do
                                             1.

some shopping.

A: Sounds good. How will we get there?

B: Let's _____. I always like to see what the public transportation
                                   2.

is like.

A: OK. After Faneuil Hall, maybe we could _____ and pick up some
                                                    3.

(Continued on next page.)

fresh fruit for later on. It's right across from there.

B: We can't. It's only open Fridays and Saturdays.

A: Oh, too bad. How about _____? We could get a "bird's-eye" view
4.

of the city that way.

B: I don't know. I'm a little afraid of heights. Why don't we _____?
5.

That way we could still see a lot of the city.

A: Fine. It'll be nice being on the water. And afterwards, how about

_____? I hear they have the largest glass-enclosed saltwater
6.

tank in the world.

B: Speaking of fish, why don't we _____ tonight?
7.

A: OK. But we'll have to go early if we don't want to wait. They don't take reservations.

B: That's no problem.

A: So we've decided what to do for breakfast and dinner. What about lunch?

B: Maybe we could _____ and have a picnic in the park. And then,
8.

how about _____? I need to buy some souvenirs, and we won't
9.

have to worry about traffic. It's a pedestrian zone.

A: I don't know. Why don't we _____? I'd really like to see some
10.

more historic sights. We can look for souvenirs tomorrow.

4. Personalization

*Imagine you are in Boston. Look at the flier in Exercise 3. Complete these
suggestions to a friend.*

1. Why don't we _____

2. How about _____

3. Let's _____

4. Maybe we could _____

5. But let's not _____

1. Affirmative Statements

*Alicia ranked the following leisure-time activities according to her preferences.
(1 = what Alicia likes most; 10 = what Alicia likes least.)*

Leisure-Time
Preferences

  __5__ cook

  __3__ watch TV

  __2__ go to the movies

  __1__ read a book

 __10__ play cards

  __9__ go for a walk

  __4__ visit friends

  __7__ talk on the phone

  __6__ eat out

  __8__ listen to music

Write about Alicia's preferences.

1. cook/eat out

   Alicia prefers *cooking to eating out.*

2. listen to music/go for a walk

   She'd rather _____

3. read a book/visit friends

   She prefers _____

4. visit friends/talk on the phone

   She prefers _____

5. watch TV/go to the movies

   She'd rather _____

6. talk on the phone/listen to music

   She'd rather _____

(Continued on next page.)

7. play cards/go to the movies

She prefers _____

8. watch TV/listen to music

She prefers _____

9. read a book/watch TV

She'd rather _____

10. play cards/read a book

She prefers _____

2. Affirmative and Negative Statements

Ralph is in the hospital. He completed this meal form.

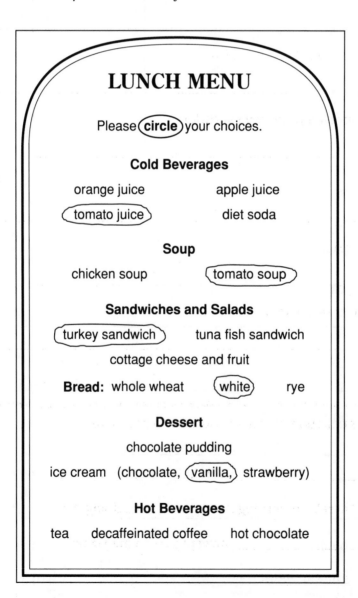

Use the cues to make sentences about Ralph's preferences.

1. He'd rather/diet soda

   He'd rather not have diet soda.

2. He'd prefer/juice

3. He'd rather/apple juice/tomato juice

4. He'd rather/a hot beverage

5. He'd prefer/chicken soup

6. He'd prefer/a sandwich/cottage cheese and fruit

7. He'd prefer/a tuna fish sandwich/a turkey sandwich

8. He'd rather/white bread

9. He'd rather/chocolate pudding

10. He'd prefer/chocolate ice cream/vanilla ice cream

3. Questions

Complete these conversations with **do you prefer, would you prefer,** *or* **would you rather**.

1. **A:** *Do you prefer* watching TV or going to the movies?

   B: It really depends. If there's something good on TV, I like doing that.

2. **A:** _____ newspapers to magazines?

   B: Oh. I definitely prefer newspapers.

(Continued on next page.)

3. **A:** I don't feel like going out.

   B: _____ stay home?

   A: Yes, I think I would.

4. **A:** I've got both vanilla and chocolate ice cream. Which _____

   have?

   B: Chocolate, please.

5. **A:** I thought we could stay home tonight.

   B: Really?

   A: _____ go out?

   B: Well, there's a good movie at the Quad.

6. **A:** There's a show at 8:00 and one at 10:00. _____ the early or

   the late show?

   B: Let's go to the early show.

7. **A:** Could you get me some juice?

   B: Sure. _____ orange or grapefruit?

   A: Orange, please.

8. **A:** How do you like to spend your free time? _____ doing things

   with friends or doing things alone?

   B: It depends. I need time for my friends, and I need time to be alone.

4. Personalization

Look at the menu in Exercise 2. Complete these sentences with true information.

1. I'd prefer _____

2. I'd rather not _____

3. I'd prefer not _____

Necessity:
Must,
Have (got) to,
Can't,
Must not,
Don't have to

▼

1. Affirmative and Negative Statements with Must

Complete these rules from the California driver's handbook. Use the words in the box with **must** *or* **must not**.

allow	drink	~~have~~	send	turn on
be	drive	place	stop	wear

1. If you are a resident of California and drive a motor vehicle on a public

   highway, you _____*must have*_____ a California driver's license.

2. You _____ your child under the age of 18 years to drive on a

   highway without a license or permit.

3. An instruction permit does not allow you to drive alone. An adult who has a

   driver's license _____ in the car with you.

4. When you move, you _____ your new address to the

   Department of Motor Vehicles in ten days.

5. You _____ so slowly that you are a danger on the road. You

   can get a ticket for driving too slowly as well as for driving too fast.

6. The law says adults _____ their children in approved safety

   seats (if a child is under 4 years old or weighs less than 40 pounds).

7. The law says you _____ your headlights when you drive from

   30 minutes after sunset until 30 minutes before sunrise, and any other time

   when you can see less than 1,000 feet ahead of you.

8. The driver of a vehicle _____ a headset over, or earplugs in,

   both ears.

9. It is illegal to leave the scene of an accident. You _____ your

   car.

2. Affirmative and Negative Statements with *Have to*

In the United States, motor vehicle rules differ from state to state. Look at the chart. Complete the statements with **have to** *or* **don't have to** *and the verbs in parentheses ( ).*

	AGE FOR LICENSE	DRIVER'S EDUCATION CLASS REQUIRED	LICENSE DURATION	FEE	ANNUAL SAFETY INSPECTION	SEAT BELT LAW
Alaska	16	No	5 yrs.	$10.00	No	Yes
California	18	No	4 yrs.	$12.00	No	Yes
Florida	16	No	4 yrs.	$20.00	No	Yes
Hawaii	18	No	4 yrs.	$20.00	No	Yes
Massachusetts	18	No	5 yrs.	$63.75	Yes	No
New York	17	Yes	4 yrs.	$17.50	Yes	Yes
Texas	16	No	4 yrs.	$16.00	Yes	Yes
Washington, D.C.	18	No	4 yrs.	$20.00	Yes	Yes

1. You _____*have to be*_____ 18 to get a California driver's license.
   (be)

2. You _____ 18 to get a license in Alaska.
   (be)

3. You _____ a driver's education class in order to get your license in
   (take)
   Florida.

4. You _____ a driver's education course in New York.
   (complete)

5. In Massachusetts, you _____ your license every four years.
   (renew)

6. In Washington, D.C., you _____ your license every four years.
   (renew)

7. You _____ a $10.00 fee for an Alaska license.
   (pay)

8. You _____ a $63.75 fee for a Massachusetts license.
   (pay)

9. You _____ your car for a yearly inspection in New York.
   (take)

10. You _____ a yearly inspection in Florida.
    (get)

11. You _____ a seat belt in Texas.
    (wear)

12. You _____ a seat belt in Massachusetts.
    (wear)

3. ▮ Contrast: Must not or Don't have to

Look again at the chart in Exercise 2. Complete these statements with **must not** *or* **don't have to.**

1. If you are under the age of 16, you _____ *must not* _____ drive in the state of California.

2. You _____ be 18 to drive in the state of Texas.

3. You _____ take a driver's education course in most of the states.

4. You _____ renew your license every four years in Massachusetts.

5. You _____ drive with an expired license.

6. You _____ pay a $20.00 license fee in Alaska.

7. You _____ have an annual car inspection in Hawaii.

8. You _____ forget to have your car inspected annually if you live in

   Washington, D.C.

9. You _____ drive without a seat belt in Florida.

10. You _____ wear a seat belt in Massachusetts.

4. ▮ Statements, Questions, and Short Answers with *Have to*

Complete these conversations. Use the correct form of **have to** *and the verbs in parentheses ( ). Use short answers when necessary. Be sure to use the correct tense.*

1. **A:** Did you pass your road test the first time you took it?

   B: No. I _____ *had to take* _____ it two more times before I passed!
                    (take)

2. **A:** _____ we _____ for gas?
                                              (stop)

   B: _____. The tank's almost empty.

3. **A:** How many times _____ you _____ public
                                                          (use)

   transportation since you moved to Los Angeles?

   B: Only once. When my car broke down.

4. **A:** _____ you _____ late yesterday?
                                            (work)

   B: _____. Luckily, I finished on time.

5. **A:** Are you thinking of buying a new car?

   B: Not yet. But in a couple of years I _____ another one.
                                           (get)
                                                                       (Continued on next page.)

6. **A:** Why didn't you come to the meeting last night?

   B: I _____ my uncle to the airport.
   (drive)

7. **A:** My wife got a speeding ticket last week.

   B: Really? How much _____ she _____?
   (pay)

   A: It was more than $100.

8. **A:** _____ your son ever _____ for a traffic
   (pay)
   violation?

   B: _____ . He's a very careful driver.

9. **A:** _____ you _____ a new license when
   (get)
   you move?

   B: _____. You can only use an out-of-state license for ten days.

10. **A:** Do you have car insurance?

    B: Of course. Everyone in New York _____ car insurance.
    (have)

5. Contrast: Must, Must not, Have to, Don't have to, and Can't

Read these test questions about road signs. Write the letter of the correct answer in the box.

1. When you see [YIELD] it means:

   a. You must come to a complete stop.
   b. You must not stop.
   c. You don't have to stop, but you must slow down and prepare
      to stop if necessary.

   ANS
   C

2. When you see [STOP] it means:

   a. You don't have to stop.
   b. You must stop.
   c. You can't stop.

   ANS

3. When you see SPEED LIMIT 50 it means:

   a. You must drive 50 miles per hour.
   b. You must not drive faster than 50 miles per hour.
   c. You don't have to drive more than 50 miles per hour.

   ANS ☐

4. When you see NO TURN ON RED it means:

   a. You have to turn when the light is red.
   b. You don't have to turn when the light is red.
   c. You must not turn when the light is red.

   ANS ☐

5. When you see DO NOT ENTER it means:

   a. You must not enter.
   b. You don't have to enter.
   c. You must enter.

   ANS ☐

6. When you see DO NOT PASS it means:

   a. You don't have to pass another car.
   b. You can't pass another car.
   c. You have to pass another car.

   ANS ☐

7. When you see ONE WAY it means:

   a. You must drive in the direction of the arrow.
   b. You must not drive in the direction of the arrow.
   c. You don't have to drive in the direction of the arrow.

   ANS ☐

8. When you see MAXIMUM SPEED 65 / MINIMUM SPEED 45 it means:

   a. You have to drive 45 miles per hour or faster.
   b. You can't drive 70 miles per hour.
   c. You don't have to drive 70 miles per hour.

   ANS ☐

6. Personalization

Complete these sentences with information about yourself.

1. Next week, I have to _____

2. I don't have to _____

3. I must not _____

4. I can't _____

34

1. Affirmative and Negative Statements with *Be Supposed to*

Today when people get married, the groom's family often shares the expenses, and older couples often pay for their own weddings. However, some people are still traditional. Read the chart and complete the sentences.

TRADITIONAL DIVISION OF WEDDING EXPENSES

Responsibilities of the Bride's Family	Responsibilities of the Groom's Family
send invitations	pay for the bride's ring
pay for food	give a rehearsal dinner
supply flowers	finance the honeymoon
pay for the groom's ring	
provide music	

1. The groom's parents ___*aren't supposed to send*___ the invitations.

2. The bride's family _____ the invitations.

3. The bride's parents _____ music.

4. The groom's family _____ the groom's ring.

5. The groom's family _____ the bride's ring.

6. The bride's parents _____ the honeymoon.

7. The groom's family _____ the honeymoon.

8. The bride's parents _____ the rehearsal dinner.

9. The groom's family _____ flowers.

10. The bride's family _____ the food.

2. Affirmative and Negative Statements with *Be Supposed to*

Linda Nelson is getting married. She completed this change of address form, but she made eight mistakes. Find the mistakes and write sentences with **was supposed to** *and* **wasn't supposed to**. *Include the number of the item.*

U.S. Postal Service CHANGE OF ADDRESS ORDER	Customer Instructions: Complete Items 1 thru 9. Except Item 8, please PRINT all information including address on face of card.	OFFICIAL USE ONLY

1. Change of address for *(Check one)* ☑ Individual   ☑ Entire Family   ☐ Business

Zone/Route ID No.

	Month	Day	Year

2. Start Date `3 0 0 6 9 5`

3. If TEMPORARY address, print date to discontinue forwarding — Month Day Year

Date Entered on Form 3982 M M D D Y Y

4. **Print** Last Name or Name of Business *(If more than one, use separate Change of Address Order Form for each)*
`L I N D A`

Expiration Date M M D D Y Y

5. **Print** First Name of Head of Household (include Jr., Sr., etc.). Leave Blank if the Change of Address Order is for a business.
`N E L S O N`

Clerk/Carrier Endorsements

6. **Print** OLD mailing address, number and street *(if Puerto Rico, include urbanization zone)*
`2 6   M A P L E   R O A D`

Apt./Suite No. `4 A`   P.O. Box No.   R.R/HCR No.   Rural Box/HCR Box No.

City `B O S T O N`   State `M A`   ZIP Code `—`

7. **Print** NEW mailing address, number and street *(if Puerto Rico, include urbanization zone)*
`2 9 8 7   C O S B Y   A V E`

Apt./Suite No.   P.O. Box No.   R.R/HCR No.   Rural Box/HCR Box No.

City `A M H E R S T`   State   ZIP Code `0 1 0 0 2 —`

8. Signature *(See conditions on reverse)*
Linda Nelson

OFFICIAL USE ONLY

9. Date Signed — Month Day Year

OFFICIAL USE ONLY
Verification Endorsement

PS Form 3575, June 1991

☆ U.S.G.P.O. 1992-309-315

1. Item ___1___ _____ *She was supposed to check one box.* _____

OR

_____ *She wasn't supposed to check two boxes.* _____

2. Item _____ _____

3. Item _____ _____

4. Item _____ _____

5. Item _____ _____

6. Item _____ _____

7. Item _____ _____

8. Item _____ _____

3. Questions and Answers with *Be Supposed to*

Linda and her new husband are on their honeymoon. Complete the conversations. Use the words in the box and **be supposed to.** *Use short answers when necessary.*

~~arrive~~	call	get	leave	shake
be	do	land	rain	tip

1. **Linda:** What time _____*are*_____ we _____*supposed to arrive*_____ in Bermuda?

   Frank: Well, the plane _____ at 10:30, but it looks like we're going to be

   late.

2. **Linda:** What time _____ we _____ to the hotel?

   Frank: Check-in time is 12:00.

3. **Linda:** _____ we _____ if we're going to be late?

   Frank: _____. We'd better look for a phone as soon as we land.

4. **Frank:** How much _____ we _____ the person who carries our

   bags?

   Linda: I think it's $1.00 a bag.

5. **Frank:** _____ the hotel restaurant _____ good?

   Linda: _____. The travel agent suggested that we go somewhere else for dinner.

6. **Linda:** What _____ we _____ with our keys when we leave the

   hotel?

   Frank: We _____ them at the front desk.

7. **Linda:** _____ it _____ today?

   Frank: _____. But look at those clouds. I think we'd better take an umbrella just in

   case.

8. **Linda:** Can you hand me that bottle of sun block?

   Frank: Sure. _____ you _____ the bottle before you use it?

   Linda: I don't know. What do the instructions say?

4.   Personalization

Complete these sentences with true information.

1. I'm supposed to _____ next week.

2. We aren't supposed to _____ in class.

3. My friend wasn't supposed to _____.

4. According to the weather forecast, it's supposed to _____

   tomorrow.

1. Affirmative and Negative Statements

Use the cues to complete this journal entry.

Thursday, July 3

I was supposed to go to the beach tomorrow, but they say it

_____ might rain _____ . I don't know what I'll
1. (might/rain)

do. I _____ shopping at the
2. (may/go)

mall, instead. It's a holiday weekend, so there

_____ some good sales. Maybe
3. (could/be)

I'll call Julie. She _____ to go
4. (might/want)

with me. On second thought, she

_____ home. She often goes
5. (may/be)

away on holiday weekends. I don't know. Shopping

_____ such a good idea. The
6. (might/be)

stores will probably be really crowded. I

_____ to a movie. There's a
7. (could/go)

Spanish movie at Cinema 8. I'm not sure. I'm afraid I

_____ enough of it. My Spanish
8. (might/understand)

really isn't that good. Maybe I'll call Ed and ask him if he

wants to take a drive to see Aunt Marla and Uncle Phil.

He _____ go. He doesn't like
9. (might/want to)

driving in the rain. Oh well, I

_____ home and read a good book.
10. (could/stay)

2. Contrast: Be Going to or Might

Read these conversations. Complete the summary sentences with **be going to** *or* **might** *and the verbs in the box.*

buy	go	rain	see	work
call	have	read	~~visit~~	write

1. **Linda:** Hello, Julie? This is Linda. Do you want to go to the mall with me?

   Julie: I don't know. I'm thinking about going to my parents'. I'm not sure. Can I call you back?

   Julie _____*might visit*_____ her parents.

2. **Julie:** What are you looking for at the mall?

   Linda: I need to get a new suit for work. I hope I can find one.

   Linda _____ a suit.

3. **Linda:** Do you think we'll get some rain?

   Carl: Definitely. Look at those clouds.

   Carl thinks it _____.

4. **Linda:** What are you doing today?

   Carl: I have tickets for a play.

   Carl _____ a play.

5. **Linda:** What are you doing this weekend?

   Sue: I'm not sure. I'm thinking about taking a drive to the country. It depends on the weather.

   Sue _____ for a ride.

6. **Linda:** Say, Ed. Do you want to see Aunt Marla and Uncle Phil tomorrow?

   Ed: I can't. I have to go into the office this weekend.

   Ed _____ this weekend.

7. **Linda:** How about dinner Saturday night?

   Ed: That's an idea. Can I call and let you know tomorrow?

   Linda and Ed _____ dinner together.

(Continued on next page.)

8. **Linda:** Hi, Aunt Marla. How are you?

   Marla: Linda! How are you? It's good to hear your voice. Listen, we just started dinner. Can I call you back?

   Linda: Sure.

   Marla: OK. I'll speak to you soon.

   Marla _____ Linda.

9. **Marla:** This is Aunt Marla. Sorry about before. What are you doing home on a holiday weekend?

   Linda: I'm tired. I just want to stay home with a good book.

   Linda _____ a book.

10. **Marla:** Do you have any other plans?

    Linda: Maybe I'll catch up on some of my correspondence.

    Linda _____ some letters.

3. Find the Mistakes

Read Linda's letter. There are four mistakes. Find and correct them.

> Dear Roberta,
>
>   How are you? It's the Fourth of July, and it's raining really hard. They say it could clear up later. Then again, it ~~could~~ ^{may} not. You never know with the weather.
>
>   Do you remember my brother, Ed? He says hi. He might has dinner with me on Saturday night. We may go to a new Mexican restaurant that opened in the mall.
>
>   I definitely might take some vacation next month. Perhaps we could do something together. It might not be fun to do some traveling. What do you think? Let me know.
>
>   Love,
>   Linda

4. Personalization

Make a short To Do list for next weekend. Put a question mark (?) next to the things you aren't sure you'll do.

To Do

Now write sentences about what you **are going to do** *and what you* **might do**.

1. _____

2. _____

3. _____

4. _____

5. _____

U N I T

36

Assumptions:
May, Might,
Could, Must,
Have to,
Have got to,
Can't

1. Affirmative and Negative Statements with *Must*

Read the facts. Complete the conclusions with **must** *or* **must not**.

1. Jack is wearing a gold wedding band on his ring finger.

   He _____*must be*_____ married.
          (be)

2. You have been calling Alicia since 8:00 P.M., but no one answers the phone.

   She _____ at home.
       (be)

3. Jackie got 98 percent on her math test.

   Her parents _____ proud of her.
         (feel)

4. Carlos works from 9:00 to 5:00 and then attends night school.

   He _____ a lot of free time.
       (have)

5. Martin works as a mechanic in Al's Automobile Shop.

   He _____ a lot about cars.
       (know)

6. Monica owns two houses and four cars.

   She _____ a lot of money.
       (have)

7. Mr. Cantor always asks me to repeat what I say.

   He _____ well.
       (hear)

8. Chen only got four hours of sleep last night.

   He _____ very tired today.
       (feel)

9. Carmen was born in Mexico and moved to the United States when she was ten.

   She _____ Spanish.
       (speak)

10. Mindy never gets good grades.

    She _____ enough.
        (study)

2. **Contrast: Must or May/Might/Could**

Circle the correct words to complete these conversations.

1. **A:** Someone broke into the Peterson's house.

   B: That's terrible! What did they take?

   A: All of Mrs. Peterson's jewelry.

   B: Oh, no. She *could*/(*must*) feel awful.

2. **A:** Is she home now?

   B: I don't know. She *might/must* be home. She sometimes gets home by 6:00.

3. **A:** Do the Petersons have insurance?

   B: Oh, they *could/must*. Mr. Peterson works at an insurance company.

4. **A:** Have you checked our burglar alarm lately?

   B: Yes. And I just put in a new battery.

   A: Good. So it *must/might* be OK.

5. **A:** Do you remember that guy we saw outside the Peterson's home last week?

   B: Yes. Why? Do you think he *might/must* be the burglar?

6. **A:** I don't know. I guess he *must/could* be the burglar. He looked a little suspicious.

   B: Maybe we should tell the police about him.

7. **A:** Someone's at the door.

   B: Who *could/must* it be?

   A: I don't know.

8. **A:** Detective Kramer wanted to ask us some questions about the burglary.

   B: Oh. It *must/could* be him. We're not expecting anybody else.

9. **A:** How old do you think Detective Kramer is?

   B: Well, he's been a detective for ten years. So he *must/might* be at least thirty-five.

10. **A:** You're right. He *couldn't/might not* be much younger than thirty-five. He probably started out

    as a police officer and became a detective in his early twenties.

    B: He looks a lot younger, though.

3. Short Answers with *Must* or *May/Might/Could*

Answer the questions.

1. **A:** Is Ron a detective?

   B: _____*He might be*_____. He always carries a notepad.

2. **A:** Does Marta speak Spanish?

   B: _____. She lived in Spain for four years.

3. **A:** Do the Taylors have a lot of money?

   B: _____. They have two homes, and they're always taking expensive

   vacations.

4. **A:** Is Ricardo married?

   B: _____. He wears a wedding ring.

5. **A:** Does Anna know Meng?

   B: _____. They both work for the same company, but there are more

   than 100 employees.

6. **A:** Is your phone out of order?

   B: _____. It hasn't rung once today, and John always calls me by this time.

7. **A:** Are Marcia and Scott married?

   B: _____. They both have the same last name, but it's possible that

   they're brother and sister.

8. **A:** Does Glenda drive?

   B: _____. She owns a car.

9. **A:** Is Oscar an only child?

   B: _____. He's never mentioned a brother or sister. I really don't know.

10. **A:** Are the Hendersons away?

    B: _____. I haven't seen them for a week, and there are no lights on in

    their apartment.

4. Contrast: Must, Could, Can't, Couldn't, Might not

Read the description of a burglary suspect and look at the four pictures.
Complete the conversation with the correct words and the names of the men
in the pictures.

21-year-old white male
short, curly blond hair
no scars or other
distinguishing features

Allen

Bob

Chet

Dave

Detective: Look at these four photos. It's possible that one of them _____*could*_____ be the

                                                   1. (must/could)

    man we're looking for. Take your time.

Witness 1: Hhmm. What do you think? _____ it be this man?

                                               2. (Could/Must)

Witness 2: It _____ be _____. He has a scar on his face. What about

          3. (can't/must)   4. (Name)

    _____? He has short blond hair and looks twenty-one.

          5. (Name)

Witness 1: I'm not sure. It _____ be. But it _____ also be

                  6. (could/must)   7. (might/must)

    _____. He also has blond hair and looks twenty-one.

          8. (Name)

Witness 2: But he has long hair.

Witness 1: The photo _____ be old. Maybe he cut it.

               9. (could/couldn't)

Witness 2: That's true. Well, it definitely _____ be _____. He's too old.

                           10. (couldn't/might not)   11. (Name)

    Maybe we could look at some more photos.

5. Personalization

Read the description of the burglar in Exercise 4. Look at these three pictures. Is one of them the burglar? What's your opinion? Complete the sentences.

Ed

Frank

George

1. It could be _____ because _____.

2. It couldn't be _____ because _____.

3. It might be _____ because _____.

1. **Kinds of Nouns**

Put these nouns into the correct category.

~~biology~~	chair	class	country	day	dollar
Election Day	furniture	hamburger	honesty	ink	Japanese
money	news	pen	president	rice	Richard
snow	snowflake	spaghetti	story	sugar	swimming
Yeltsin	zoo				

PROPER NOUNS

_____   _____

_____   _____

COMMON NOUNS

Count   Non-count

                          biology

_____   _____

_____   _____

_____   _____

_____   _____

_____   _____

_____   _____

_____   _____

_____   _____

_____   _____

_____   _____

2. Count and Non-count Nouns

Complete these food facts. Use the correct form of the words in parentheses ( ).

1. ___Chocolate___ ___has___ a chemical that creates a feeling similar to being in love.
    (Chocolate)   (have)

2. _____ _____ the second most popular food in the United States.
    (Potato)   (be)

    _____ _____ the first.
    (Rice)   (be)

3. _____ _____ Americans' favorite snack food.
    (Potato chip)   (be)

4. _____ _____ more potato chips than any other _____ in
    (American)   (eat)   (people)
    the world.

5. Chewing raw onions for five minutes _____ all the germs in your mouth.
                                        (kill)

6. _____ _____ at least 5,000 years old.
    (Popcorn)   (be)

7. _____ _____ really nuts. They are members of the bean family.
    (Peanut)   (not be)

8. _____ _____ been around for just a little over a hundred years. It's a
    (Peanut butter) (have)
    relatively new health-food invention.

9. The _____ of the hot dog _____ very long. It began 3,500 years ago.
        (history)   (be)

10. _____ _____ the favorite dessert in the United States.
    (Ice cream)   (be)

Source: Elkort, Martin E., *The Secret Life of Food: A Feast of Food and Drink, Folklore and Fact*, 1991, J.P. Tarcher, Los Angeles.

3. Much or Many

Complete this food quiz. Use **much** *or* **many**. *Then try to answer the questions.*

1. How ___much___ Vitamin C does an onion have? As ___much___ as

ⓐ two apples

b. one orange

c. three carrots

2. How _____ rolls are there in a "baker's dozen"?

a. eleven

b. twelve

c. thirteen

3. How _____ pasta does an American eat each year?

a. two pounds

b. sixteen pounds

c. fifty-five pounds

4. How _____ pounds of pasta does an Italian eat each year?

a. sixteen

b. fifty-five

c. eighty

5. How _____ food does the average American eat each year?

a. 1,400 pounds

b. 2,400 pounds

c. 3,400 pounds

6. How _____ money does the average American household spend on

vegetables each week?

a. $10.26

b. $5.34

c. $2.13

7. How _____ cups of coffee does the average American drink each day?

a. 3.4

b. 4.4

c. 2.4

8. How _____ ice cream does the United States produce a year?

a. 1.5 quarts per person

b. 5.1 quarts per person

c. 15 quarts per person

Sources: Elkort, Martin E., *The Secret Life of Food: A Feast of Food and Drink, Folklore and Fact,* 1991, J.P. Tarcher, Los Angeles.

Conn, Charis and Hena Silverman (eds.), *What Counts: The Complete Harper's Index,* 1991, Harper's Magazine, New York.

4.   Quantifiers

Circle the correct words in italics to complete the conversation.

A: How was the party?

B: It was good. I saw (*a lot of*) / *much* people from my childhood.
1.

A: That's nice. Were there *many/much* family members there too?
2.

B: No. Unfortunately a *few/few* relatives live nearby, so not *many/much* could come.
3.   4.

A: How was the food?

B: Delicious! In fact, there's so *many/much* left over, you should come by tonight. I can show you
5.

the photos, too. *Several/A great deal of* people had cameras with them, and we got *some/a little*
6.   7.

pictures back already.

A: That was fast!

B: Yeah. We brought them to one of those places where you only have to wait *a few/few* hours to
8.

get them back.

A: Great! What time should I come over?

B: Let's see. I get out of school at 5:00, and I don't think I'll have *a little/much* homework tonight.
9.

How about 7:00?

A: Will that give you *enough/many* time to get ready?
10.

B: Sure. There's really nothing to do.

A: OK. See you then.

1. Definite and Indefinite Articles

Circle the correct choice in italics to complete these conversations that take place in school. If you don't need an article, circle Ø.

1. **A:** Can I borrow *a*/*the* pen?

   B: Sure. Take *a/the* one on *a/the* desk. I don't need it.

2. **A:** Is *a/the* teacher here yet?

   B: No, she hasn't come yet.

3. **A:** What do you think of Mr. Mencz?

   B: He's *a/the* best teacher I've ever had.

4. **A:** Have you done *the/Ø* homework?

   B: Yes. But I don't think I got *a/the* last answer right.

5. **A:** Could you open *a/the* window, please?

   B: Which one?

   A: *A/The* one next to *a/the* door.

   B: Sure.

6. **A:** Who's that?

   B: That's *a/the* school principal.

   A: Oh, I've never seen her before.

7. **A:** Do you like *the/Ø* history?

   B: It's OK. But I prefer *the/Ø* science.

8. **A:** We learned about *an/the* ozone layer in science class yesterday.

   B: Did you know there's *a/the* hole in it?

   A: Yeah. It's pretty scary.

9. **A:** What kind of work do you do?

   B: I'm *an/the* engineer. What about you?

   A: I'm *a/Ø* mechanic.

(Continued on next page.)

10. **A:** Are they *some/Ø* students?

    B: I don't think so. They look like *the/Ø* teachers.

11. **A:** Do you know where I can get *some/the* water around here?

    B: Sure. There's *a/the* water fountain right across *a/the* hall, right next to *the/Ø* rest rooms.

12. **A:** Do you know what *a/the* homework is for tomorrow?

    B: We have to read *a/the* fable.

    A: Which one?

    B: *A/The* one on page 23.

2.   Definite and Indefinite Articles

Complete the conversation. Use **a/an** *or* **the** *when necessary.*

Bing Yang: Hi, Georgina. What are you doing?

Georgina: I'm reading _____*a*_____ fable for my English class.
                           1.

Bing Yang: What's _____ fable? I've never heard the word before.
                      2.

Georgina: _____ fable is _____ short story about _____ animals.
        3.   4.   5.

Bing Yang: About _____ animals? Like _____ science story?
          6.   7.

Georgina: No. It's _____ fiction. _____ animals act like _____ people.
         8.   9.   10.

      They usually teach _____ lesson. _____ lesson is called
                         11.   12.

      _____ moral of _____ story, and it always comes at _____ end.
      13.   14.   15.

Bing Yang: That's interesting. Who's _____ author of _____ fable you're reading?
                      16.   17.

Georgina: Aesop. He was _____ ancient Greek writer.
            18.

Bing Yang: Oh, now I know what you're talking about. My parents used to read _____ fables
                                                19.

      to me when I was _____ child.
                  20.

Georgina: Well, they're also good for _____ adults. I'll lend you _____ book when I'm
                           21.   22.

      finished, if you're interested.

Bing Yang: Thanks. I am.

3. Definite and Indefinite Articles

Complete this version of an Aesop's fable. Use **a/an** *or* **the** *when necessary.*

The Fox and the Goat

_____*A*_____ fox fell into _____ well and couldn't get out again. Finally, _____ thirsty
   1.   2.   3.
goat came by and saw _____ fox in _____ well. "Is _____ water good?"
                              4.   5.   6.
_____ goat asked. "Good?" said _____ fox. "It's _____ best water I've ever tasted
   7.   8.   9.
in my whole life. Why don't you come down and try it?"

_____ goat was very thirsty, so he jumped into _____ well. When he was finished
   10.   11.
drinking, he looked for _____ way to get out of _____ well, but, of course, there wasn't
                              12.   13.
any. Then _____ fox said, "I have _____ excellent idea. Stand on your back legs and
              14.   15.
place your front legs firmly against _____ front side of _____ well. Then, I'll climb onto
                                          16.   17.
your back and, from there, I'll step on your horns and be able to get out. When I'm out, I'll help you get

out, too." _____ goat thought this was _____ good idea and followed _____
              18.   19.   20.
advice.

When _____ fox was out of _____ well, he quickly and quietly walked away.
           21.   22.
_____ goat called loudly after him and reminded him of _____ promise he had made to
   23.   24.
help him out. But _____ fox turned and said, "You should have as much sense in your head as
                      25.
you have _____ hairs in your beard. You jumped into _____ well before making sure you
              26.   27.
could get out again."

Moral: Look before you leap.

UNIT 1 Present Progressive

ANSWER KEY

Where the full form is given, the contraction is also acceptable. Where the contracted form is given, the full form is also acceptable.

1

2. getting 3. trying 4. planning 5. having 6. doing 7. matching 8. grabbing 9. giving 10. saying 11. visiting 12. forgetting 13. hurrying 14. beginning 15. deciding 16. answering 17. happening 18. determining 19. entertaining 20. continuing

2

POSTCARD 1

2. is shining 3. is blowing 4. are flying 5. are building

POSTCARD 2

1. are traveling 2. 'm standing/am standing 3. is getting 4. is taking 5. 's starting/is starting

POSTCARD 3

1. 'm studying/am studying 2. living 3. is improving 4. 're helping/are helping 5. 'm trying/am trying

3

POSTCARD 1

2. **A:** Is it raining? **B:** No, it isn't. 3. **A:** Are the children building sand castles? **B:** Yes, they are.

POSTCARD 2

4. **A:** Are Susan and Rick traveling in Spain? **B:** No, they aren't. 5. **A:** Is the sun shining? **B:** No, it isn't. 6. **A:** Is Molly taking pictures? **B:** Yes, she is.

POSTCARD 3

7. **A:** Is Elise practicing her French? **B:** Yes, she is. 8. **A:** Is she enjoying her summer? **B:** Yes, she is. 9. **A:** Is she working? **B:** No, she isn't.

4

2. The sun isn't shining. It's raining. 3. Smoke isn't coming from the second-floor windows. It's coming from the fourth/top-floor windows. 4. The fire fighter isn't carrying a man down the ladder. He's carrying a woman down the ladder 5. Three more fire engines aren't arriving at the scene. One more fire engine is arriving at the scene.

5

2. are you watching 3. 's reporting/is reporting 4. 's happening/is happening 5. are the fire fighters doing 6. are they taking them 7. are the victims doing

UNIT 2 Simple Present Tense

1

2. studies 3. works 4. hopes 5. lives 6. reaches 7. rushes 8. knows 9. marries 10. pays 11. calls 12. swims 13. happens 14. does 15. says 16. has 17. tries 18. buys 19. goes 20. passes

2

3. Mario and Silvia go to school. 4. Mario and Silvia have lunch. 5. Mario studies at the library. Silvia plays basketball. 6. Mario goes home. Silvia visits her grandmother. 7. Mario and Silvia do (their) homework. 8. Mario has dinner. Silvia practices the guitar. 9. Mario plays computer games. Silvia makes dinner. 10. Mario reads the newspaper. Silvia washes the dishes.

3

2. **A:** Do Mario and Silvia get up at the same time? **B:** Yes, they do. 3. **A:** Does Silvia watch TV in the morning? **B:** No, she doesn't. 4. **A:** Does she listen to the radio? **B:** Yes, she does. 5. **A:** Does Mario study at the library? **B:** Yes, he does. 6. **A:** Does he do his homework at school? **B:** No, he doesn't. 7. **A:** Does Silvia play basketball? **B:** Yes, she does. 8. **A:** Does Mario play computer games before dinner? **B:** No, he doesn't. 9. **A:** Do Mario and Silvia eat dinner together? **B:** No, they don't. 10. **A:** Does Silvia wash the dishes after dinner? **B:** Yes, she does.

4

2. Silvia is usually on time. 3. Silvia and Mario never miss school. 4. Silvia and Mario always do their homework. 5. Mario is often tired. 6. The students usually eat lunch in school. 7. They are always hungry. 8. Silvia rarely gets up late.

5

2. What do you do before the show? (Before the show) I talk to the TV audience. 3. How long do you talk to the audience? (I talk to the audience) for half an hour/a half hour. 4. When do you tape the show? (I tape the show) at 5:30/from 5:30 to 6:30. 5. How long does the show last?

(It lasts) an hour. 6. Where do you go after the show? (After the show) I go home. 7. What do you do at home? I work in the garage. 8. When do you write new jokes? (I write new jokes) at 10:00 P.M./between 10:00 P.M. and 12:00 A.M. 9. How long do you work with other writers? (I work with other writers) for four hours. 10. How many hours do you sleep? (I sleep) four hours.

6

2. He doesn't talk to them after each show. He talks to them before each show. 3. The *Night Show* doesn't last a half hour. It lasts an hour. 4. He doesn't write screenplays for two hours. He writes jokes. 5. They don't meet for three hours. They meet for four hours.

U N I T 3 Contrast: Simple Present Tense and Present Progressive

1

3. She reads 4. She is drinking/She's drinking 5. She wears 6. She eats 7. She wants 8. She speaks 9. She seems 10. She is going/She's going

2

2. drives 3. takes 4. is taking/'s taking 5. are repairing 6. is using 7. takes 8. moves 9. is slowing down 10. is raining/'s raining 11. drives 12. is listening to 13. listens to 14. is describing 15. doesn't want 16. is moving 17. likes 18. feels 19. knows 20. has

3

2. I am having	⟶	I have
3. I'm liking	⟶	I like
4. we are speaking	⟶	we speak
5. class is meeting	⟶	class meets
6. I'm not knowing	⟶	I don't know
7. What do you do	⟶	What are you doing
8. Do you still look	⟶	Are you still looking

U N I T 4 Imperative

1

2. Look down. 3. Don't lean backward. 4. Don't breathe in. 5. Keep you eyes shut. 6. Don't wear tight clothes. 7. Don't turn the lights off. 8. Turn the music up. 9. Put the air conditioner on low. 10. Don't come late.

2

3. Walk 4. ride 5. Go 6. Don't turn 7. make 8. Continue 9. stop 10. Don't cross 11. be 12. Don't pass 13. Have 14. Don't work

U N I T 5 Simple Past Tense

1

3. caught 4. did 5. looked 6. found 7. gave 8. hurried 9. saw 10. died 11. kissed 12. came 13. lived 14. met 15. needed 16. opened 17. put 18. read 19. said 20. thought 21. understood 22. voted 23. won 24. felt 25. was...were

2

2. was 3. weren't...were 4. wasn't 5. was 6. wasn't...was 7. wasn't...was 8. was...wasn't 9. were 10. were

3

2. A: Where was Simone de Beauvoir from? **B:** She was from France. **3. A:** What nationality was Pablo Neruda? **B:** He was Chilean. **4. A:** Who was Boccaccio? **B:** He was a poet and storyteller. **5. A:** Was Agatha Christie French? **B:** No, she wasn't. **6. A:** What nationality was Lorraine Hansberry? **B:** She was American. **7. A:** Was Honoré de Balzac a poet? **B:** No, he wasn't. **8. A:** When was Karel Čapek born? **B:** He was born in 1890. **9. A:** Who was Isaac Babel? **B:** He was a short-story writer and playwright.

4

Biography 1

2. spent **3.** wrote **4.** included **5.** translated **6.** died

Biography 2

1. was **2.** lived **3.** began **4.** called **5.** had **6.** painted

Biography 3

1. were **2.** built **3.** flew **4.** watched **5.** took place **6.** lasted

5

2. A: What did he do? **B:** He was a writer./He wrote books and translated other people's works. **3. A:** Did he write poetry? **B:** No, he didn't. **4. A:** Where did he spend most of his life? **B:** (He spent most of his life) in the United States. **5. A:** What did people call Anna Mary Robertson Moses? **B:** (They called her) Grandma Moses. **6. A:** What did she do? **B:** She was a painter./She painted. **7. A:** When did she begin painting? **B:** She began painting in her seventies. **8. A:** Did she have formal art training? **B:** No, she didn't. **9. A:** Where did the Wright brothers build their first planes? **B:** (They built their first planes) in their bicycle shop in Ohio. **10. A:** Did both brothers fly the *Flyer 1*? **B:** No, they didn't. **11. A:** Where did the first controlled flight take place? **B:** (It took place) near Kitty Hawk, North Carolina. **12. A:** How long did the flight last? **B:** (It lasted) only about 12 seconds.

6

3. Orville didn't have serious health problems. **4.** Wilbur didn't grow a moustache. **5.** Orville didn't lose most of his hair. **6.** Wilbur didn't take courses in Latin. **7.** Wilbur didn't like to play jokes. **8.** Wilbur didn't dress very fashionably. **9.** Wilbur didn't play the guitar. **10.** Orville didn't build the first glider. **11.** Orville didn't make the first attempts to fly. **12.** Orville didn't choose the location of Kitty Hawk. **13.** Wilbur didn't have a lot of patience. **14.** Wilbur didn't live a long life.

UNIT 6 Used to

1

2. People used to read **3.** People used to cook **4.** People used to fly **5.** People used to have **6.** People used to wash **7.** People used to use **8.** It used to take

2

2. didn't use to work **3.** didn't use to have **4.** used to take **5.** didn't use to be **6.** used to live **7.** didn't use to like **8.** didn't use to know **9.** used to return **10.** used to write

3

2. A: Where did she use to live? **B:** She used to live in New York. **3. A:** What did she use to do? **B:** She used to be a student. **4. A:** Did she use to have long hair? **B:** Yes, she did. **5. A:** Did she use to wear glasses? **B:** No, she didn't. **6. A:** Did she use to be married? **B:** Yes, she did.

UNIT 7 Past Progressive and Simple Past Tense

1

2. wasn't writing **3.** was answering **4.** were eating **5.** weren't eating **6.** was attending **7.** weren't writing **8.** were discussing **9.** wasn't answering **10.** was returning

2

2. A: What was he doing at 9:30? **B:** He was meeting with Ms. Jacobs. **3. A:** Was Mr. Cotter writing police reports at 10:30? **B:** No, he wasn't. **4. A:** What kind of reports was he writing? **B:** He was writing financial reports. **5. A:** What was he doing at 11:30? **B:** He was answering correspondence. **6. A:** Was he having lunch at 12:00? **B:** Yes, he was. **7. A:** Who was eating lunch with him? **B:** Mr. Webb was eating lunch with him. **8. A:** Where were they having lunch? **B:** They were having lunch at Sol's Cafe. **9. A:** Who was he talking to at 3:30? **B:** He was talking to Allen. **10. A:** What were they discussing? **B:** They were discussing the budget.

3

3. were visiting **4.** took place **5.** killed **6.** injured **7.** took
8. exploded **9.** went out **10.** stopped **11.** started **12.** were
eating **13.** shook **14.** occurred **15.** crumbled **16.** collapsed
17. arrived **18.** found **19.** was walking **20.** went off **21.** had
22. were carrying **23.** were riding **24.** went out **25.** stopped
26. had to **27.** reached **28.** was waiting **29.** drove **30.** was
happening

4

2. What happened when the bomb exploded? **3.** What were
the school children doing when the lights went out? **4.** How
many people were working in the building when the bomb
exploded? **5.** What were they doing when the bomb went
off? **6.** What happened to the offices when the blast
occurred? **7.** What was he doing when the bomb exploded?
8. What happened when the rescue workers brought him to
the ambulance?

UNIT 8 Wh- Questions: Subject and Predicate

1

2. Whose phone rang at midnight? **3.** Who was calling for
Megan? **4.** Who was having a party? **5.** How many people
left the party? **6.** What surprised them? **7.** Whose friend
called the police? **8.** How many police arrived?

2

2. How many rooms does her apartment have? (f.) **3.** How
much rent does she pay? (j.) **4.** When does she pay the
rent? (c.) **5.** Who(m) does she live with? (h.) **6.** What does
she do? (g.) **7.** Which company does she work for? (d.)
8. How long does she plan to stay there? (a.) **9.** How does
she get to work? (b.) **10.** Why does she take the bus? (i.)

3

2. Why did you leave Chicago? **3.** Who moved with you?
4. Where did you get a job? **5.** When did it start? **6.** How
many rooms does it have? **7.** How many of the rooms came
with carpeting? **8.** How much do you each pay? **9.** What do
you need to buy? **10.** Whose brother wants to visit her?
11. Who called last Sunday? **12.** Who(m) did you speak to?
13. When do they want to visit you? **14.** Why is there plenty
of room?

UNIT 9 Future

1

2. She is going to/She's going to wash the car. **3.** They are
going to/They're going to get gas. **4.** She is going to/She's
going to make a left turn. **5.** She is going to/She's going to
get a ticket. **6.** They are going to/They're going to crash.
7. They are going to/They're going to eat lunch. **8.** It is
going to/It's going to rain.

2

2. How long are you going to stay? **3.** Are you going to stay
at a hotel? **4.** What are you going to do in San Francisco?
5. Are you going to visit Fisherman's Wharf? **6.** Is your
daughter going to go with you? **7.** What is he going to do?
8. When are you going to leave?

3

2. He isn't going to take the train. He's going to/He is going
to fly/take a plane. **3.** He isn't going to travel alone. He's
going to/He is going to travel with his wife. **4.** The Medinas
aren't going to leave from Chicago. They're going to/They
are going to leave from New York. **5.** They aren't going to
fly US Air. They're going to/They are going to fly FairAirs.
6. They aren't going to leave on July 11. They're going
to/They are going to leave on June 11. **7.** The plane isn't
going to depart at 7:00 A.M. It's going to/It is going to depart
at 7:00 P.M. **8.** Mrs. Medina isn't going to sit in seat 15B.
She's going to/She is going to sit in seat 15C.

4

2. will **3.** will become **4.** Will...replace **5.** won't replace
6. will...operate **7.** will...do **8.** will/'ll be **9.** will/'ll sing
10. will/'ll dance **11.** Will...tell **12.** will **13.** won't...be
14. will...do **15.** Will...have **16.** will **17.** will...help **18.** won't
19. will/'ll perform **20.** won't **21.** will improve **22.** will lose
23. will create **24.** Will...need **25.** will...look **26.** won't look
27. will/'ll resemble **28.** will...happen **29.** will/'ll happen

5

Next Wednesday <u>is</u> the first performance of *Bats*. Melissa Robins <u>is playing</u> the leading role. Robins, who lives in Italy and who is vacationing in Greece, is not available for an interview at this time. She <u>is</u>, however, <u>appearing</u> on Channel 8's *Theater Talk* sometime next month.

Although shows traditionally begin at 8:00 P.M., *Bats*, because of its length, <u>starts</u> a half hour earlier.

Immediately following the opening-night performance, the company <u>is having</u> a reception in the theater lounge. Tickets are still available. Call 555–6310 for more information.

6

2. I'm going to do 3. I'll ask 4. It's going to rain 5. are they showing 6. we're going to have 7. I'll take 8. We're going to arrive 9. are we going to get 10. We'll take 11. We're landing 12. are you going to stay

UNIT 10 Future Time Clauses

1

2. is…'ll drink (c.) 3. finish…'ll do (g.) 4. washes…'ll dry (e.) 5. get in…'ll fasten (d.) 6. gets…'ll drive (b.) 7. stops …'ll use (f.) 8. is…'ll be (a.)

2

2. will apply…before…finishes 3. After…finishes…'ll visit 4. While…works…'ll take 5. 'll visit…before…gets 6. When…finishes…'ll fly 7. 'll get married…when …'s 8. 'll return…after…gets married

3

2. retire 3. will…go 4. have 5. turn 6. will want 7. visit 8. won't want

4

2. Vera saves enough money from her summer job, she's going to buy a plane ticket. 3. Vera goes home, she's going to buy presents for her family. 4. Vera arrives at the airport, her father will be there to drive her home. 5. Vera and her father get home, they'll have dinner. 6. Vera will give her family the presents…they finish dinner. 7. Vera's brother will wash the dishes…Vera's sister dries them. 8. The whole family will stay up talking…the clock strikes midnight. 9. they go to bed, they'll all feel very tired. 10. Vera will fall asleep…her head hits the pillow.

UNIT 11 Present Perfect: For and Since

1

2. looked 3. come 4. brought 5. played 6. had 7. gotten 8. fallen 9. watched 10. lost 11. won 12. eaten

2

FOR: ten years, a day, an hour, a long time, many months
SINCE: 4:00 P.M., Monday, yesterday, she was a child

3

BIOGRAPHY 1
2. for 3. Since 4. has written 5. has begun 6. been 7. since 8. gone 9. since

BIOGRAPHY 2
1. has been 2. for 3. has appeared 4. since 5. Since 6. has received 7. has directed 8. has formed

BIOGRAPHY 3
1. have been 2. for 3. Since 4. have had 5. have made 6. have sold 7. Since 8. have become

4

2. A: How many novels has she written since 1970? B: She has written five novels since 1970. 3. A: Has she received any awards since her Pulitzer Prize for Literature? B: Yes, she has. 4. A: How long has Jodie Foster been an actress? B: (She has been an actress) for most of her life. 5. A: Has she won any Oscars since 1988? B: Yes, she has. 6. A: Has she directed any movies since she graduated from Yale? B: Yes, she has. 7. A: Have The New Kids on the Block been a pop music group for more than twenty years? B: No, they haven't. 8. A: How long have they been successful in the United States? B: (They have been successful in the United States) for the last ten years/since—. 9. A: Have they had any U.S. Top 10 entries since their first U.S. hit? B: Yes, they have.

5

3. Min Ho has won three awards 4. Marilyn has appeared in two movies 5. Victor hasn't seen Marilyn since 1989. 6. Andreas has lost three games

UNIT 12 Present Perfect: Already and Yet

1

2. acted 3. given 4. kept 5. held 6. traveled 7. sung
8. danced 9. fought 10. known 11. drunk 12. smiled

2

3. Has she gone food shopping yet? She's already gone food shopping. 4. Has she given the patient medication yet? She's already given the patient medication. 5. Has she called the doctor for the blood-test results yet? She hasn't called the doctor for the blood-test results yet./She hasn't yet called the doctor for the blood test results. 6. Has she changed the patient's bandages yet? She's already changed the patient's bandages. 7. Has she given the patient a bath yet? She hasn't given the patient a bath yet./She hasn't yet given the patient a bath. 8. Has she taken the patient's temperature yet? She's already taken the patient's temperature. 9. Has she done the laundry yet? She hasn't done the laundry yet./She hasn't yet done the laundry. 10. Has she exercised the patient's legs yet? She hasn't exercised the patient's legs yet./She hasn't yet exercised the patient's legs.

3

2. have already made progress → has already made progress
3. hasn't walked already → hasn't walked yet
4. Already she has gained three pounds → She has already gained three pounds./She has gained three pounds already.
5. Have you decide yet? → Have you decided yet?

UNIT 13 Present Perfect: Indefinite Past

1

2. begun 3. forgiven 4. promised 5. gone 6. felt 7. grown
8. heard 9. seen 10. decided 11. kept 12. acted

2

2. has chosen 3. have come 4. have been 5. have not been
6. has…been 7. has worked 8. have…read 9. have/'ve rejected 10. have gone 11. have…felt 12. have gotten
13. have not/haven't gotten 14. have…told 15. have played
16. has produced 17. have…been 18. have…seen

3

2. How many nominations for Best Actor have you received? 3. Have you ever seen your own films? 4. Have you ever gone to the Academy Awards? 5. How many foreign films have you acted in?/How many times have you acted in foreign films? 6. Have you ever worked with Sophia Loren? 7. How has it changed your life? 8. Have you read any good scripts lately?

UNIT 14 Contrast: Present Perfect and Simple Past Tense

1

2. Joe had 3. Joe got 4. Joe has made 5. Joe has been 6. Joe looked 7. Joe bought 8. Joe has paid 9. Joe has read 10. Joe felt

2

2. got 3. have/'ve been 4. did…have 5. became 6. had
7. were 8. did…last 9. divorced 10. Did…have 11. didn't
12. have/'ve remained 13. saw 14. have become 15. Has…remarried 16. hasn't 17. did…fail 18. got 19. didn't know
20. did…meet 21. were 22. did…move 23. have/'ve lived

3

2. began 3. got 4. had 5. was 6. has risen 7. occurred 8. has created 9. began 10. had 11. were 12. has…increased
13. stayed 14. got 15. has changed

4

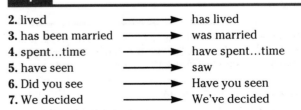

2. lived ⟶ has lived
3. has been married ⟶ was married
4. spent…time ⟶ have spent…time
5. have seen ⟶ saw
6. Did you see ⟶ Have you seen
7. We decided ⟶ We've decided

Present Perfect Progressive

1

2. Amanda has been working at the *Daily News* since 1994/for—years. **3.** She has/She's been writing a series about the homeless for a month/since last month. **4.** The number of homeless Americans has been increasing since 1980/for—years. **5.** Pete has been working at a homeless shelter for a month/since last month. **6.** He has/He's been studying economics for a year/since last year. **7.** Amanda and Pete have been looking for a new apartment for two months.

2

2. hasn't been sleeping **3.** hasn't been eating **4.** has been/'s been studying **5.** hasn't been working **6.** has been/'s been raining **7.** has been/'s been running **8.** hasn't been waiting **9.** have been/'ve been trying **10.** haven't been feeling

3

2. How long has the police officer been standing **3.** How long has the woman been walking **4.** How long have the children been playing **5.** How long has...been raining **6.** How long have the men been waiting for

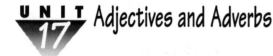 **Contrast: Present Perfect and Present Perfect Progressive**

1

2. has been selling **3.** has been fighting **4.** have opened **5.** has...done **6.** has been appearing **7.** has been traveling **8.** has received **9.** has started **10.** has written **11.** has...combined

2

2. have...been **3.** have...been doing **4.** 've been reading **5.** Have...read **6.** 've seen **7.** Have...bought **8.** 've been using **9.** has...opened **10.** 've been opening

3

2. How much money has her business made this year? **3.** How long has she been traveling around the world? **4.** How many countries has she visited? **5.** How many copies of her book has she sold? **6.** Has she written any books since *Body and Soul?* **7.** Has she ever appeared on TV? **8.** How long have she and her husband lived in England?/ How long have she and her husband been living in England?

Adjectives and Adverbs

1

2. nice **3.** fast **4.** well **5.** dangerous **6.** beautifully **7.** hard **8.** safely **9.** occasional **10.** happy **11.** sudden **12.** carefully **13.** angrily **14.** unfortunate

2

2. Good news travels fast! **3.** It has five large rooms, **4.** it's in a very large building. **5.** It's not too bad. **6.** It seems pretty quiet. **7.** the landlord speaks very loudly. **8.** He doesn't hear well. **9.** Was it a hard decision? **10.** We had to decide quickly. **11.** I have to leave now. **12.** Good luck with your new apartment.

3

2. hard **3.** well **4.** nice **5.** extremely **6.** comfortable **7.** cold **8.** pretty **9.** friendly **10.** safe **11.** really **12.** important **13.** late **14.** completely **15.** empty **16.** good **17.** easily **18.** near **19.** frequently **20.** wonderful

4

2. disturbed **3.** entertaining **4.** disgusted **5.** inspiring **6.** paralyzed **7.** moving **8.** moved **9.** frightening **10.** disturbed **11.** astonishing **12.** frightening **13.** bored **14.** disappointed **15.** touching **16.** exciting **17.** entertaining **18.** bored

UNIT 18 Adjectives: Equatives and Comparatives

1

2. more expensive **3.** hotter **4.** bigger **5.** better **6.** more difficult **7.** prettier **8.** more beautiful **9.** worse **10.** longer **11.** farther/further **12.** more careful **13.** more dangerous **14.** earlier

2

2. larger **3.** slower **4.** bigger than **5.** more quiet/quieter **6.** more expensive **7.** cheaper than **8.** better **9.** more convenient **10.** farther **11.** faster **12.** more comfortable

3

2. Y...cheaper than...X. **3.** Y...larger than...X. **4.** Y...heavier than...X. **5.** X...more efficient than...Y. **6.** Y...more effective than...X. **7.** Y...faster than...X. **8.** X...noisier than...Y. **9.** Y...better than...X. **10.** X...worse than...Y.

4

2. not as big as **3.** not as cold as **4.** as hot as **5.** not as wet as **6.** not as windy as **7.** not as sunny as

5

2. The smaller the city, the lower the crime rate. **3.** The warmer the climate, the busier the police. **4.** The colder the weather, the greater the number of robberies. **5.** The larger the police force, the more violent the city. **6.** The later in the day, the higher the number of car thefts. **7.** The higher the unemployment rate, the higher the crime rate. **8.** The more mobile the population, the more dangerous the city. **9.** The more organized the community, the safer the neighborhood.

6

2. is getting less and less crowded. **3.** is getting lower and lower. **4.** is getting higher and higher. **5.** are getting more and more expensive. **6.** are getting less and less dangerous. **7.** is getting more and more violent. **8.** are getting more and more crowded.

UNIT 19 Adjectives: Superlatives

1

2. the funniest **3.** the biggest **4.** the most wonderful **5.** the best **6.** the worst **7.** the happiest **8.** the most important **9.** the warmest **10.** the most interesting **11.** the farthest/furthest **12.** the most intelligent **13.** the slowest **14.** the most expensive

2

2. The least expensive **3.** Funji **4.** the most expensive **5.** Minon **6.** the lowest **7.** Minon **8.** the smallest **9.** the lightest **10.** the most powerful **11.** the heaviest **12.** Minon **13.** the most convenient **14.** Rikon **15.** the least important

3

2. the smallest **3.** the tallest **4.** the longest **5.** the farthest **6.** the busiest **7.** the most popular **8.** the fastest **9.** the slowest **10.** the most expensive

UNIT 20 Adverbs: Equatives, Comparatives, Superlatives

1

2. faster	the fastest
3. more beautifully	the most beautifully
4. sooner	the soonest
5. more dangerously	the most dangerously
6. better	the best
7. earlier	the earliest
8. more carefully	the most carefully
9. worse	the worst
10. farther/further	the farthest/the furthest

2

2. harder than **3.** more slowly/slower than **4.** faster **5.** more accurately **6.** more aggressively than **7.** worse than **8.** better **9.** more successfully **10.** more seriously **11.** more regularly than

Winning Team Members: Bob, Randy, Dennis
Losing Team Members: Alex, Rick, Larry, Elvin

3

2. ran as fast as **3.** jumps as high as **4.** didn't jump as high as **5.** didn't throw the discus as far as **6.** threw the discus as far as **7.** didn't do as well as **8.** didn't compete as successfully as

4

2. E…the slowest/the most slowly…slower/more slowly than **3.** higher than…B **4.** E…the highest **5.** farther than…E **6.** E…the farthest **7.** E…the best

5

2. She's running more and more frequently. **3.** He's throwing the ball farther and farther. **4.** She's shooting more and more accurately. **5.** He's jumping higher and higher. **6.** He's running slower and slower/more and more slowly. **7.** They're skating more and more gracefully. **8.** They're practicing harder and harder.

6

2. more slow	⟶	slower/more slowly
3. the farthest	⟶	the farther
4. more frequent	⟶	more frequently
5. more quick	⟶	more quickly
6. as fast than	⟶	as fast as
7. long	⟶	longer

UNIT 21 Gerunds: Subject and Object

1

2. going **3.** meeting **4.** Sitting **5.** running **6.** lifting **7.** doing **8.** taking **9.** Exercising **10.** wasting

2

2. lifting weights **3.** dancing **4.** Doing situps **5.** lifting weights **6.** Dancing **7.** Walking **8.** dancing **9.** doing situps/playing tennis/jogging **10.** doing situps/playing tennis/jogging

3

2. dislikes doing **3.** enjoys dancing **4.** mind teaching **5.** kept practicing **6.** denied/denies stepping **7.** considering taking **8.** regrets not beginning **9.** suggests going **10.** admits feeling

UNIT 22 Gerunds after Prepositions

1

2. of **3.** to **4.** on **5.** in **6.** for/to **7.** of **8.** in **9.** about **10.** to

2

2. succeeded in collecting **3.** is worried about missing **4.** are used to working **5.** believe in talking **6.** are tired of waiting **7.** insists on reaching **8.** approves of having **9.** are opposed to going **10.** looking forward to returning

3

2. striking **3.** firing **4.** permitting **5.** being **6.** getting **7.** missing **8.** trying **9.** making **10.** hearing

UNIT 23 Infinitives after Certain Verbs

1

2. want to see **3.** refuses to go **4.** threatened to end **5.** hesitate/am hesitating to take **6.** seems to be **7.** attempted to create **8.** intend to stay **9.** needs to speak **10.** will agree to go

2

2. to do the dishes…him to do the dishes. **3.** her to buy some milk…to buy some milk. **4.** him to drive her to her aunt's…to drive her to her aunt's. **5.** him to have dinner at her place …to have dinner at her place. **6.** him to give her his answer…to give her his answer. **7.** to cut his hair…her to cut his hair. **8.** him to be home at 7:00…to be home at 8:00.

UNIT 24 Infinitive of Purpose

1

3. She used her credit card in order not to pay right away.
4. I asked for the dressing room (in order) to try on a dress.
5. They went to the snack bar (in order) to get a drink.
6. I'm going to wait for a sale (in order) to save some money. **7.** She tried on the blouse (in order) to be sure of the size. **8.** He only took fifty dollars with him in order not to spend more. **9.** They went to Lacy's on Monday in order not to miss the sale. **10.** She asked the salesclerk to show her the scarf (in order) to feel the material.

2

2. (in order) to return **3.** in order not to pay **4.** (in order) to carry **5.** (in order) to sign **6.** to have **7.** (in order) to cut **8.** (in order) to find out **9.** in order not to miss **10.** in order not to waste

UNIT 25 Infinitives with *Too* and *Enough*

1

2. It's too noisy for me to concentrate. **3.** The work is varied enough to be interesting. **4.** The salary is high enough for me to support my family. **5.** My desk is too small to hold all my things. **6.** I can sleep late enough to feel awake in the morning. **7.** My boss speaks too quickly for me to understand him. **8.** The bookshelves aren't low enough for me to reach.

+ 1, 3, 4, 6
− 2, 5, 7, 8

2

2. late enough to call **3.** too heavy for me to carry **4.** too sweet to drink **5.** small enough to fit **6.** too noisy for me to think **7.** not old enough to retire **8.** not hot enough to need **9.** not sick enough to call **10.** too high for me to reach

3

for to think	→ to think/for me to think
for me to lift it	→ for me to lift
too strong	→ strong enough
too get out	→ to get out
enough good	→ good enough

UNIT 26 Contrast: Gerunds and Infinitives

1

3. to leave **4.** walking **5.** to be **6.** to look **7.** taking **8.** to ask **9.** living **10.** seeing

2

2. is tired of being **3.** quit drinking **4.** believes in working **5.** forgot to bring **6.** remember locking **7.** stopped to get **8.** afford to move **9.** refuses to live **10.** intends to get **11.** agreed to help **12.** offered to drive

3

3. being cautious is wise. **4.** It's dangerous to walk on ice. **5.** It's a good idea to install a burglar alarm. **6.** Being afraid all the time isn't good. **7.** It's risky to walk alone on a dark, deserted street. **8.** It's helpful to work together.

UNIT 27 Ability: Can, Could, Be able to

1

3. can read an English newspaper…could read one
4. couldn't read an English novel…can't read one. **5.** can speak on the phone…couldn't speak on the phone.
6. couldn't speak with a group of people…can speak with a group of people. **7.** couldn't write a social letter…can write one. **8.** Before the course he couldn't write a business letter, and he still can't write one. **9.** He can order a meal in English now, and he could order a meal in English before, too. **10.** He can go shopping now, and he could go shopping before, too.

Summary: Fernando can do a lot more now than he could do before the course.

2

2. A: What languages can you speak? **3. A:** Could you speak Spanish when you were a child? **B:** No, I couldn't. **4. A:** Could you speak French? **B:** Yes, I could. **5. A:** Before you came here, could you understand spoken English? **B:** No, I couldn't. **6. A:** Can you understand song lyrics? **B:** Yes, I can. **7. A:** Before this course, could you write a business letter in English? **B:** No, I couldn't. **8. A:** could you drive a car before you came here? **B:** No, I couldn't. **9. A:** Can you drive a car now? **B:** No, I can't. **10. A:** What can you do now that you couldn't do before? **B:** can do…couldn't do

3

2. are able to interpret **3.** are not able to distinguish **4.** are not able to understand **5.** are able to hear **6.** have been able

to regain **7.** are able to read **8.** is not able to recognize **9.** is not able to work **10.** are able to communicate

4

2. A: Will she be able to hear **B:** Yes, she will. **3. A:** Will she be able to hear **B:** No, she won't. **4. A:** Will she be able to hear **B:** Yes, she will. **5. A:** Will she be able to hear **B:** Yes, she will.

5

2. could read **3.** could not/couldn't accept **4.** was able to learn **5.** was able to accept **6.** could see **7.** will…be able to do **8.** can do **9.** can do **10.** has been able to master **11.** has been able to speak **12.** will be able to get

6

I wasn't able understand	I wasn't able to understand
I could leave	I was able to leave
I can to understand	I can understand
I can practice a lot	I've been able to practice a lot
She can explains	She can explain
I can do even more	I will be able to do even more

7

(Answers will vary.)

UNIT 28 Permission: May, Could, Can, Do you mind if…?

1

2. c. **3.** b. **4.** h. **5.** f. **6.** a. **7.** e. **8.** g.

2

2. we (please) review Unit 6 (please)? **3.** I (please) borrow your pen (please)? **4.** I look at your (class) notes? **5.** I come late to the next class? **6.** my husband (please) come to the next class with me (please)? **7.** I (please) ask a question (please)? **8.** we (please) use a dictionary (please)? **9.** we

(please) leave five minutes early (please)? **10.** my sister goes on the class trip with the rest of the class?

3

2. can bring **3.** can't/cannot drink **4.** can pay **5.** can pay **6.** may not pay **7.** may not purchase **8.** can't/cannot get

4

(Answers will vary.)

UNIT 29 Requests: Will, Would, Could, Can, Would you mind...?

1

2. a **3.** f. **4.** h. **5.** c. **6.** b. **7.** g. **8.** e.

Requests granted: 3, 4, 5, 6, 8.
Requests refused: 1, 7.

2

2. opening the window **3.** mail a letter **4.** pick up a sandwich **5.** staying late tonight **6.** keep the noise down **7.** come to my office **8.** get Frank's phone number **9.** explaining this note to me **10.** lend me $5.00

3

(Note 3) Will you return please the stapler? → Will you please return the stapler?/Will you return the stapler, please?
(Note 5) Would you mind leave → Would you mind leaving
(Note 6) Could you please remember to lock the door. → Could you please remember to lock the door?

4

(Answers will vary.)

UNIT 30 Advice: Should, Ought to, Had better

1

3. What should I wear? **4.** Should I bring a gift? **5.** No, you shouldn't. **6.** Should I bring something to eat or drink? **7.** You should bring something to drink. **8.** When should I respond? **9.** You should respond by May 15. **10.** Should I call Aunt Rosa? **11.** No, you shouldn't. **12.** Who(m) should I call? **13.** You should leave a message at 555-3234.

2

2. You'd better not leave **3.** You'd better not arrive **4.** You'd better write **5.** You'd better dress **6.** You'd better not chew **7.** You'd better not ask **8.** You'd better thank **9.** You'd better go **10.** You'd better have

3

2. you should/ought to/'d better wear **3.** Should I tell **4.** You'd better/ought to/should wait **5.** Should I offer **6.** They should/ought to pay **7.** Should I write **8.** should I send **9.** You should/ought to/'d better wait **10.** I'd better not forget **11.** Should I call **12.** You'd better call

4

(Answers will vary.)

UNIT 31 Suggestions: Let's, How about...? Why don't...? Why not...?

1

2. a. **3.** b. **4.** g. **5.** j. **6.** e. **7.** i. **8.** f. **9.** d. **10.** h.

2

2. Maybe you could .
3. Let's .
4. How about ?
5. Why don't you ?
6. Let's .
7. Maybe we could .
8. Why don't you ?
9. How about ?
10. That's a good idea .

3

2. take the "T" **3.** go to Haymarket **4.** taking an elevator to the top of the John Hancock Observatory **5.** take a boat excursion **6.** going to the New England Aquarium **7.** eat at Legal Seafoods **8.** walk along the waterfront **9.** going shopping in Downtown Crossing **10.** walk the Freedom Trail

4

(Answers will vary.)

UNIT 32 Preferences: Prefer, Would prefer, Would rather

1

2. listen to music than go for a walk. **3.** reading a book to visiting friends. **4.** visiting friends to talking on the phone. **5.** go to the movies than watch TV. **6.** talk on the phone than listen to music. **7.** going to the movies to playing cards. **8.** watching TV to listening to music. **9.** read a book than watch TV. **10.** reading a book to playing cards.

2

2. He'd prefer (to have) juice. **3.** He'd rather have tomato juice than apple juice. **4.** He'd rather not have a hot beverage. **5.** He'd prefer not to have chicken soup. **6.** He'd prefer a sandwich to cottage cheese and fruit. **7.** He'd prefer a turkey sandwich to a tuna fish sandwich. **8.** He'd rather have white bread. **9.** He'd rather not have chocolate pudding. **10.** He'd prefer vanilla ice cream to chocolate ice cream.

3

2. Do you prefer **3.** Would you rather **4.** would you rather **5.** Would you rather **6.** Would you prefer **7.** Would you prefer **8.** Do you prefer

4

(Answers will vary.)

UNIT 33 Necessity: Must, Have (got) to, Can't, Must not, Don't have to

1

2. must not allow **3.** must be **4.** must send **5.** must not drive **6.** must place **7.** must turn on **8.** must not wear **9.** must stop

2

2. don't have to be **3.** don't have to take **4.** have to complete **5.** don't have to renew **6.** have to renew **7.** have to pay **8.** have to pay **9.** have to take **10.** don't have to get **11.** have to wear **12.** don't have to wear

3

2. don't have to **3.** don't have to **4.** don't have to **5.** must not **6.** don't have to **7.** don't have to **8.** must not **9.** must not **10.** don't have to

4

2. A: Do…have to stop **B:** Yes, we do **3. A:** have…had to use **4. A:** Did…have to work **B:** No, I didn't **5. B:** 'll have to get **6. B:** had to drive **7. B:** did…have to pay **8. A:** Has…had to pay **B:** No, he hasn't **9. A:** Will/Do…have to get **B:** Yes, I will/do **10. B:** has to have

5

2. b. **3.** b. **4.** c. **5.** a. **6.** b. **7.** a. **8.** b.

6

(Answers will vary.)

UNIT 34 Expectations: Be supposed to

1

2. is supposed to send **3.** are supposed to provide **4.** isn't supposed to pay for **5.** is supposed to pay for **6.** aren't supposed to finance **7.** is supposed to finance **8.** aren't supposed to give **9.** isn't supposed to supply **10.** is supposed to pay for

2

2. Item 2. She was supposed to write the month first./She wasn't supposed to write the day first. **3.** Item 4. She was supposed to print/write her last name./She wasn't supposed to print/write her first name. **4.** Item 5. She was supposed to print/write her first name./She wasn't supposed to print/write her last name. **5.** Item 6. She was supposed to write/include her zip code. **6.** Item 7. She was supposed to write her state. **7.** Item 8. She was supposed to sign her name./She wasn't supposed to print her name. **8.** Item 9. She was supposed to write the date.

3

1. F: is/was supposed to land **2.** L: are...supposed to get **3.** L: Are...supposed to call F: Yes, we are **4.** F: are...supposed to tip **5.** F: Is...supposed to be F: No, it isn't **6.** L: are...supposed to do F: are supposed to leave **7.** L: Is...supposed to rain F: No, it isn't **8.** F: Are...supposed to shake

4

(Answers will vary.)

UNIT 35 Future Possibility: May, Might, Could

1

2. may go **3.** could be **4.** might want **5.** may not be **6.** might not be **7.** could go **8.** might not understand **9.** might not want to **10.** could stay

2

2. might buy **3.** is going to rain **4.** is going to see **5.** might go **6.** is going to work **7.** might have **8.** is going to call **9.** is going to read **10.** might write

3

might has ⟶ might have
I definitely might ⟶ I definitely am going to
might not be ⟶ might be

4

(Answers will vary.)

UNIT 36 Assumptions

1

2. must not be **3.** must feel **4.** must not have **5.** must know **6.** must have **7.** must not hear **8.** must feel **9.** must speak **10.** must not study

2

2. might **3.** must **4.** must **5.** might **6.** could **7.** could **8.** must **9.** must **10.** couldn't

3

2. She must **3.** They must **4.** He must be **5.** She might **6.** It must be **7.** They might be **8.** She must **9.** He might be **10.** They must be

4

2. Could **3.** can't **4.** Bob **5.** Chet **6.** could **7.** might **8.** Dave **9.** could **10.** couldn't **11.** Allen

5

(Answers will vary.)

UNIT 37 Nouns and Quantifiers

1

Proper nouns: Election Day, Japanese, Richard, Yeltsin
Common count nouns: chair, class, country, day, dollar, hamburger, pen, president, snowflake, story, zoo
Common non-count nouns: furniture, honesty, ink, money, news, rice, snow, spaghetti, sugar, swimming

2

2. Potatoes are...Rice is **3.** Potato chips are **4.** Americans eat...people **5.** kills **6.** Popcorn is **7.** Peanuts are not **8.** Peanut butter has **9.** history...is **10.** Ice cream is

3

2. many (c.) **3.** much (b.) **4.** many (b.) **5.** much (a.) **6.** several (c.) **7.** many (a.) **8.** much (c.)

4

2. many **3.** few **4.** many **5.** much **6.** Several **7.** some **8.** a few **9.** much **10.** enough

UNIT 38 Articles: Definite and Indefinite

1

1. the...the **2.** the **3.** the **4.** the...the **5.** a...The...the **6.** the
7. Ø...Ø **8.** the...a **9.** an...a **10.** Ø...Ø **11.** some...a...the...the
12. the...a...The

2

2. a **3.** A **4.** a **5.** Ø **6.** Ø **7.** a **8.** Ø **9.** The **10.** Ø **11.** a **12.** The
13. the **14.** the **15.** the **16.** the **17.** the **18.** an **19.** Ø **20.** a
21. Ø **22.** the

3

2. a **3.** a **4.** the **5.** the **6.** the **7.** the **8.** the **9.** the **10.** The
11. the **12.** a **13.** the **14.** the **15.** an **16.** the **17.** the **18.** The
19. a **20.** the **21.** the **22.** the **23.** The **24.** the **25.** the **26.** Ø
27. the

TEST: UNITS 1–4

PART ONE

DIRECTIONS: Circle the letter of the correct answer to complete each sentence.

Example:

Jackie never _____ coffee. A Ⓑ C D

  A. drink

  B. drinks

  C. is drinking

  D. was drinking

1. At the moment, Meng _____ on a report. A B C D

  A. doesn't work

  B. is working

  C. work

  D. works

2. Water _____ at 100°C. A B C D

  A. boil

  B. boiling

  C. boils

  D. is boiling

3. What _____ these days? A B C D

  A. are you doing

  B. do you do

  C. you are doing

  D. you do

4. Do you have any aspirin? George _____   A   B   C   D

a headache.

A. are having

B. has

C. have

D. is having

5. Alicia _____ to the park every day.   A   B   C   D

A. does

B. go

C. goes

D. is going

6. When you get to the corner, _____ left.   A   B   C   D

A. is turning

B. turn

C. turning

D. turns

7. Walk! _____ run!   A   B   C   D

A. Don't

B. No

C. Not

D. You don't

8. Jennifer never _____ in the ocean.　　A　B　C　D

A. is swimming

B. swim

C. swimming

D. swims

9. A: Do you like spaghetti?　　　　　　　　　A　B　C　D

　　B: Yes, I _____.

A. am

B. do

C. don't

D. like

PART TWO

*DIRECTIONS: Each sentence has four underlined words or phrases. The four underlined parts of the sentence are marked A, B, C, and D. Circle the letter of the **one** underlined word or phrase that is NOT CORRECT.*

Example:

Ana <u>rarely</u> <u>is drinking</u> coffee, but <u>this morning</u> she　　A　Ⓑ　C　D
　　　A　　　B　　　　　　　　　　C

<u>is having</u> a cup.
　D

10. Terry <u>usually</u> <u>drives</u> to work, but <u>today</u> she <u>takes</u>　　A　B　C　D
　　　　　A　　　B　　　　　　　C　　　D

　　the train.

11. Carlos <u>usually</u> doesn't <u>eat</u> pizza, but <u>at</u> the moment　　A　B　C　D
　　　　　　A　　　　　B　　　　　C

　　he <u>is wanting</u> a slice.
　　　　D

12. Frank <u>rarely</u> <u>goes</u> downtown because he <u>doesn't</u>　　A　B　C　D
　　　　　A　　B　　　　　　　　　　　C

　　<u>likes</u> the crowded streets.
　　D

13. Ana <u>usually</u> <u>is eating</u> in the cafeteria, but <u>these days</u>
          A   B   C
she <u>is eating</u> in the park.
     D

A   B   C   D

14. <u>What</u> <u>you are</u> <u>studying</u> these days <u>at school</u>?
      A   B   C   D

A   B   C   D

15. Jackie <u>don't</u> <u>speak</u> French, but <u>she's</u> <u>studying</u> Spanish
          A   B   C   D
at the Adult Center.

A   B   C   D

16. Julie <u>loves</u> tennis, but <u>rarely she</u> <u>plays</u> because she
        A   B   C
<u>doesn't have</u> time.
   D

A   B   C   D

17. <u>Stand</u> up straight, <u>breathe</u> deeply, <u>hold</u> your head up,
     A   B   C
and <u>no look</u> down.
     D

A   B   C   D

18. John <u>works always</u> late and <u>is</u> <u>rarely</u> home before
           A   B C
8:00 <u>at night</u>.
      D

A   B   C   D

19. I <u>know</u> you usually <u>don't wear</u> a jacket, but <u>wear</u> one
    A   B   C
today because it <u>is feeling</u> cold outside.
            D

A   B   C   D

20. A breeze <u>is blowing</u>, the <u>sun</u> <u>shines</u>, and the sky <u>looks</u>
            A   B   C   D
clear and bright.

A   B   C   D

TEST: UNITS 5–8

▼

PART ONE

DIRECTIONS: Circle the letter of the correct answer to complete each sentence.

Example:

Jackie never _____ coffee.   A Ⓑ C D

  A. drink

  B. drinks

  C. is drinking

  D. was drinking

1. Roger _____ me at 9:00 last night.   A B C D

A. called

B. calls

C. is calling

D. was calling

2. There _____ a lot of people in the   A B C D

  park yesterday.

A. are

B. is

C. was

D. were

3. One day last March, I _____ a very   A   B   C   D

strange letter.

A. did get

B. got

C. used to get

D. was getting

4. Where _____ to school?   A   B   C   D

A. did you go

B. you did go

C. you go

D. you went

5. Claude didn't _____ in Canada.   A   B   C   D

A. lived

B. use to live

C. used to live

D. used to living

6. Rick left class early because he _____   A   B   C   D

a headache.

A. had

B. have

C. used to have

D. was having

7. _____ is your English teacher?   A   B   C   D

A. Who

B. Whom

C. Whose

D. Why

8. Who _____ yesterday at the store?   A   B   C   D

A. did you see

B. did you use to see

C. you saw

D. you were seeing

9. As soon as the light turned red, she   A   B   C   D

_____ the car.

A. did stop

B. stopped

C. stops

D. was stopping

10. They _____ when the phone rang.   A   B   C   D

A. sleep

B. slept

C. was sleeping

D. were sleeping

11. Johnny _____ the paper when

I interrupted him.

A. read

B. reads

C. was reading

D. were reading

A   B   C   D

12. **A:** Who _____ there?

B: Mr. Jackson saw me.

A. did you see

B. saw you

C. you saw

D. you see

A   B   C   D

13. **A:** Whose teacher _____?

B: I called Jack's teacher.

A. called you

B. did you call

C. you called

D. were calling

A   B   C   D

PART TWO

DIRECTIONS: Each sentence has four underlined words or phrases. The four underlined parts of the sentence are marked A, B, C, and D. Circle the letter of the <u>one</u> underlined word or phrase that is NOT CORRECT.

Example:

Ana <u>rarely</u> <u>is drinking</u> coffee, but <u>this morning</u> she
    A   B   C

<u>is having</u> a cup.
   D

A   Ⓑ   C   D

14. Paul <u>was</u> <u>drying</u> the dishes <u>when</u> he <u>was dropping</u>
       A   B   C   D

the plate.

A   B   C   D

15. When Gloria <u>were</u> a little girl, she <u>used to</u> <u>pretend</u>
                A   B   C

    that she <u>had</u> a horse.
              D

    A   B   C   D

16. What <u>did</u> you <u>used to</u> <u>do</u> when you <u>felt</u> afraid?
              A   B   C   D

    A   B   C   D

17. <u>As soon as</u> the alarm clock <u>rang</u>, she <u>woke up</u> and
           A   B   C

    <u>was getting</u> out of bed.
       D

    A   B   C   D

18. Once <u>when</u> I <u>was</u> a little boy, I <u>used to get</u> sick and
               A   B   C

    <u>went</u> to the hospital.
     D

    A   B   C   D

19. Who <u>you did</u> <u>see</u> when you <u>left</u> the building <u>last night</u>?
              A   B   C   D

    A   B   C   D

20. <u>While</u> I <u>drove</u> home, I <u>turned on</u> the car radio and
          A   B   C

    <u>heard</u> the news about the accident.
     D

    A   B   C   D

TEST: UNITS 9–10

PART ONE

DIRECTIONS: Circle the letter of the correct answer to complete each sentence.

Example:

Jackie never _____ coffee. **A** **Ⓑ** **C** **D**

A. drink

B. drinks

C. is drinking

D. was drinking

1. It _____ tomorrow. **A** **B** **C** **D**

A. rains

B. rained

C. 's going to rain

D. 's raining

2. Don't eat so much. You _____ sick later. **A** **B** **C** **D**

A. 're feeling

B. feel

C. felt

D. 'll feel

3. The package will _____ tomorrow. **A** **B** **C** **D**

A. arrive

B. arrives

C. arriving

D. be going to arrive

4. What _____ you do next month when

you finish this course?

A. are

B. did

C. do

D. will

A   B   C   D

5. Goodnight. I _____ tomorrow.

A. 'll see you

B. 'm going to see you

C. 'm seeing you

D. see

A   B   C   D

6. Mike and I _____ to the Crash

concert. We already have our tickets.

A. are going

B. go

C. went

D. will go

A   B   C   D

7. What will Michiko do when she _____

her license?

A. gets

B. is getting

C. is going to get

D. will get

A   B   C   D

8. That driver _____ a speeding ticket.   A   B   C   D

The police are right behind him.

A. gets

B. is getting

C. is going to get

D. will get

9. The car of the future _____ on electricity.   A   B   C   D

A. is running

B. ran

C. runs

D. will run

10. According to this schedule, the next train   A   B   C   D

_____ in ten minutes.

A. leave

B. leaves

C. left

D. leaving

11. **A:** Will you be home tomorrow night?   A   B   C   D

B: No, _____.

A. I don't

B. I'm not

C. I will

D. I won't

12. I'll see you _____.   **A   B   C   D**

A. at the moment

B. in an hour

C. last night

D. usually

13. **A:** Why did you borrow those chairs from Jimmy?   **A   B   C   D**

     B: I _____ a party next Saturday night.

A. had

B. have

C. 'm going to have

D. 'll have

14. **A:** Call me when you get home.   **A   B   C   D**

     B: Don't worry. I _____.

A. don't forget

B. forget

C. 'm not forgetting

D. won't forget

PART TWO

DIRECTIONS: Each sentence has four underlined words or phrases. The four underlined parts of the sentence are marked A, B, C, and D. Circle the letter of the <u>one</u> underlined word or phrase that is NOT CORRECT.

Example:

Ana <u>rarely</u> <u>is drinking</u> coffee, but <u>this morning</u> she   **A   Ⓑ   C   D**
    A   B   C
<u>is having</u> a cup.
  D

15. When Marie <u>will get</u> <u>home</u>, she <u>is going to</u> <u>call</u> me.   **A   B   C   D**
               A   B   C   D

16. <u>As soon as</u> she <u>finds</u> a new <u>job</u>, she <u>tells</u> her boss.   **A**   **B**   **C**   **D**
      A   B   C   D

17. <u>I'll make</u> some sandwiches <u>before</u> <u>I'll leave</u> for the   **A**   **B**   **C**   **D**
      A   B   C
office <u>in the morning</u>.
           D

18. According to the weather <u>forecast</u>, it <u>going to be</u> hot   **A**   **B**   **C**   **D**
                           A   B
and sunny <u>tomorrow</u> with a chance of a thunderstorm
             C
<u>in the afternoon</u>.
     D

19. The doors <u>will</u> open <u>until</u> the train <u>comes</u> to a   **A**   **B**   **C**   **D**
            A   B   C
complete <u>stop</u>.
        D

20. My sister <u>is going to</u> <u>be</u> sixteen <u>next</u> month, and she   **A**   **B**   **C**   **D**
             A   B   C
<u>has</u> a big party with all her friends.
  D

TEST: UNITS 11–16

PART ONE

DIRECTIONS: Circle the letter of the correct answer to complete each sentence.

Example:

Jackie never _____ coffee.   A Ⓑ C D

  A. drink

  B. drinks

  C. is drinking

  D. was drinking

1. Anita _____ in Texas since 1991.   A B C D

  A. is living

  B. has lived

  C. have lived

  D. lived

2. John has already _____ this course.   A B C D

  A. been taking

  B. taken

  C. takes

  D. took

3. The journalist hasn't finished the   A   B   C   D

article _____.

A. already

B. now

C. then

D. yet

4. The department store has been in business   A   B   C   D

_____ many years.

A. already

B. for

C. in

D. since

5. How many cups of coffee have you   A   B   C   D

_____ this morning?

A. been drinking

B. drank

C. drink

D. drunk

6. Sheila _____ New Mexico six years ago.   A   B   C   D

A. has been leaving

B. has left

C. left

D. used to leave

7. They have been _____ lunch in the   A   B   C   D

same cafeteria for ten years.

A. ate

B. eat

C. eaten

D. eating

8. The Jordans _____ at R & J Corp.   A   B   C   D

since 1992.

A. are working

B. has been working

C. have been working

D. worked

9. Have you read any good books _____?   A   B   C   D

A. already

B. ever

C. lately

D. now

10. It's _____ all day.   A   B   C   D

A. is raining

B. has been raining

C. has rained

D. rained

11. A: Has the mail come yet? A B C D

    B: Yes, it _____.

A. did

B. has

C. have

D. is

12. I'm sorry I'm late. How long _____? A B C D

A. did you wait

B. have you been waiting

C. have you waited

D. you have been waiting

13. A: What are you doing? A B C D

    B: I _____ on this report all morning.

A. 'm working

B. 've been working

C. 've worked

D. worked

14. _____ you cut your hair lately? A B C D

A. Are

B. Did

C. Has

D. Have

PART TWO

DIRECTIONS: Each sentence has four underlined words or phrases. The four underlined parts of the sentence are marked A, B, C, and D. Circle the letter of the one underlined word or phrase that is NOT CORRECT.

Example:

Ana <u>rarely</u> <u>is drinking</u> coffee, but <u>this morning</u> she
    A   B   C
<u>is having</u> a cup.
  D

        A   Ⓑ   C   D

15. <u>When</u> she <u>was</u> a child, she <u>has worked</u> in a factory
     A   B   C
<u>for</u> more than three years.
  D

        A   B   C   D

16. Erik <u>have</u> <u>been sleeping</u> <u>for</u> more than <u>three hours</u>.
        A   B   C   D

        A   B   C   D

17. Last night we <u>have rented</u> two <u>videos</u> and <u>watched</u>
               A   B   C
them with some <u>friends</u>.
          D

        A   B   C   D

18. Jack <u>hasn't done</u> a thing <u>since</u> he <u>has gotten</u> to work.
       A   B   C   D

        A   B   C   D

19. <u>Since</u> I <u>have known</u> Tommy, he <u>had</u> three
    A   B   C
different <u>jobs</u>.
       D

        A   B   C   D

20. She <u>hasn't</u> <u>washed</u> the dishes or <u>made</u> the
        A   B   C
beds <u>already</u>.
    D

        A   B   C   D

TEST: UNITS 17–20

PART ONE

DIRECTIONS: Circle the letter of the correct answer to complete each sentence.

Example:

Jackie never _____ coffee.　　　　　　　A　Ⓑ　C　D

　A. drink

　B. drinks

　C. is drinking

　D. was drinking

1. I have _____ boss in the world.　　　　A　B　C　D

A. a good

B. best

C. the best

D. the better

2. Jessica is an excellent employee. She works　　　　A　B　C　D

_____, and she's very dependable.

A. as hard

B. hard

C. harder than

D. hardly

3. The apple pie smells _____.   A   B   C   D

A. more wonderfully

B. the most wonderfully

C. wonderful

D. wonderfully

4. The larger the apartment, the _____   A   B   C   D

the rent.

A. expensive

B. expensively

C. more expensive

D. most expensive

5. That's _____ story I have ever heard.   A   B   C   D

A. a ridiculous

B. the ridiculous

C. the more ridiculous

D. the most ridiculous

6. This living room isn't as _____ ours.   A   B   C   D

A. big as

B. bigger

C. bigger than

D. biggest

7. Stella drives more _____ Phil.   **A   B   C   D**

A. careful as

B. carefully as

C. careful than

D. carefully than

8. Is there anything else on TV? This show doesn't   **A   B   C   D**

seem _____.

A. interested

B. interesting

C. interestingly

D. more interested

9. Riding in a car is more dangerous   **A   B   C   D**

_____ flying.

A. as

B. from

C. than

D. that

10. Please call if you're going to arrive   **A   B   C   D**

_____.

A. as late

B. late

C. lately

D. later than

11. It's getting more and _____ to find

    a cheap apartment.

  A. difficult

  B. less difficult

  C. more difficult

  D. more difficult than

                                     A   B   C   D

12. She plays the piano _____ as she sings.

  A. as beautiful

  B. as beautifully

  C. more beautifully

  D. the most beautifully

                                     A   B   C   D

PART TWO

DIRECTIONS: Each sentence has four underlined words or phrases. The four underlined parts of the sentence are marked A, B, C, and D. Circle the letter of the <u>one</u> underlined word or phrase that is NOT CORRECT.

Example:

Ana <u>rarely</u> <u>is drinking</u> coffee, but <u>this morning</u> she
    A   B   C

<u>is having</u> a cup.
  D

                                     A   Ⓑ   C   D

13. Today will be <u>colder</u>, <u>wetter</u>, and <u>windier</u>
                  A   B   C

    <u>that</u> yesterday.
    D

                                       A   B   C   D

14. This <u>nice</u> <u>new</u> apartment looks <u>perfectly</u> for a
        A   B   C

    <u>young</u> couple.
    D

                                       A   B   C   D

15. Our <u>new</u> telephone-answering machine doesn't
        A

    operate as <u>quiet</u> <u>as</u> our <u>old</u> one.
             B   C   D

16. The clothes at Brooks are <u>nicer</u>, <u>interesting</u>,
  A   B
and <u>less expensive</u> <u>than</u> the clothes at
  C   D
B & S Department Store.

A   B   C   D

17. This is the <u>more interesting</u> and the <u>funniest</u> book
  A   B
I have <u>ever</u> <u>read</u>.
  C   D

A   B   C   D

18. Thompson controlled the ball <u>the best</u>, kicked the
  A
ball <u>the farthest</u>, and ran the <u>faster</u> <u>of</u> all the players.
  B   C   D

A   B   C   D

19. The critic was <u>amused</u> by the <u>funny</u> story line, but
  A   B
she found the acting <u>extremely</u> <u>unexcited</u>.
  C   D

A   B   C   D

20. It's getting <u>easy</u> and <u>easier</u> to find a <u>good</u>
  A   B   C
<u>inexpensive</u> color TV.
  D

A   B   C   D

TEST: UNITS 21–26

PART ONE

DIRECTIONS: Circle the letter of the correct answer to complete each sentence.

Example:

Jackie never _____ coffee. A Ⓑ C D

  A. drink

  B. drinks

  C. is drinking

  D. was drinking

1. Do you enjoy _____? A B C D

A. swim

B. swimming

C. the swimming

D. to swim

2. I'm looking forward to _____ on vacation. A B C D

A. be going

B. go

C. going

D. have gone

3. The doctor advised Mike to stop _____. A B C D

A. for smoking

B. smoke

C. smoking

D. to smoke

4. She's going on a diet in order _____

weight.

A. for not gaining

B. not for gaining

C. not to gain

D. to gain not

A   B   C   D

5. I'm excited _____ starting my new job.

A. about

B. for

C. of

D. to

A   B   C   D

6. Maria is not used to _____ alone.

A. live

B. lives

C. lived

D. living

A   B   C   D

7. Have you ever considered _____ jobs?

A. change

B. changed

C. changing

D. to change

A   B   C   D

8. Where did he use to _____?   A   B   C   D

A. live

B. lived

C. lives

D. living

9. Meng is interested _____ to college.   A   B   C   D

A. for going

B. in going

C. to go

D. to going

PART TWO

DIRECTIONS: *Each sentence has four underlined words or phrases. The four underlined parts of the sentence are marked A, B, C, and D. Circle the letter of the* __one__ *underlined word or phrase that is NOT CORRECT.*

Example:

Ana <u>rarely</u> <u>is drinking</u> coffee, but <u>this morning</u> she   A   Ⓑ   C   D
    A   B   C

<u>is having</u> a cup.
  D

10. <u>Collecting</u> <u>stamps</u> <u>are</u> <u>a</u> popular hobby.   A   B   C   D
     A   B   C D

11. Jackie needs a ladder because she is <u>not</u> <u>enough tall</u>   A   B   C   D
                     A   B

  <u>to</u> <u>reach</u> the top shelf.
  C D

12. When <u>do</u> you <u>expect</u> <u>him</u> <u>being</u> here?   A   B   C   D
       A   B   C   D

13. <u>Before</u> <u>leaving</u> the office, please <u>remember</u> <u>locking</u>   A   B   C   D
    A   B   C   D

  the door.

14. Fran <u>enjoys</u> <u>dancing</u> and always looks forward
     A   B

    <u>to</u> <u>learn</u> the latest dances.
    C D

       A   **B**   **C**   **D**

15. After <u>moving</u> to Canada, Monica had to get <u>used</u> <u>to</u> <u>do</u>
        A   B   C D

    everything in English.

       A   **B**   **C**   **D**

16. Sue was so excited <u>about</u> <u>winning</u> the contest that
                 A   B

    she <u>forgot</u> <u>meeting</u> her husband at the restaurant.
        C   D

       A   **B**   **C**   **D**

17. Scott <u>didn't run</u> fast <u>enough</u> <u>for</u> <u>win</u> the race.
       A   B   C D

       A   **B**   **C**   **D**

18. Erica <u>avoids</u> <u>going</u> <u>to</u> parties because she has trouble
        A   B C

    <u>to remember</u> people's names.
    D

       A   **B**   **C**   **D**

19. <u>To do</u> situps <u>is</u> hard work, and many people don't
    A   B

    <u>enjoy</u> <u>doing</u> them.
    C   D

       A   **B**   **C**   **D**

20. Jimmy's father forced <u>him</u> <u>to apologize</u> <u>of</u> <u>breaking</u>
                     A   B   C   D

    the window.

       A   **B**   **C**   **D**

TEST: UNITS 27–36

PART ONE

DIRECTIONS: Circle the letter of the correct answer to complete each sentence.

Example:

Jackie never _____ coffee.   A Ⓑ C D

  A. drink

  B. drinks

  C. is drinking

  D. was drinking

1. A: Would you shut the door please?   A B C D

    B: _____

  A. Certainly.

  B. No, I can't.

  C. Yes, I could.

  D. Yes, I would.

2. Why _____ a movie tonight?   A B C D

  A. about seeing

  B. don't we see

  C. not seeing

  D. we don't see

3. Marcia can't speak German yet, but after a few lessons   **A**   **B**   **C**   **D**

she _____ speak a little.

A. can

B. could

C. is able to

D. will be able to

4. In 1992, Kristi Yamaguchi _____ win   **A**   **B**   **C**   **D**

the gold medal in figure skating at the Winter

Olympics.

A. can

B. could

C. will be able to

D. was able to

5. According to the law, everyone must   **A**   **B**   **C**   **D**

_____ a license in order to drive.

A. has

B. have

C. have to

D. to have

6. _____ rain tomorrow?   **A**   **B**   **C**   **D**

A. Is it going to

B. May it

C. Should it

D. Would it

7. I _____ make new friends since
   I moved here.   A   B   C   D

A. can't

B. couldn't

C. haven't been able to

D. 'm not able to

8. I _____ arrive on time, so please start
   dinner without me.   A   B   C   D

A. could

B. may

C. may not

D. should

9. Jamie prefers working at home _____
   working in an office.   A   B   C   D

A. more

B. than

C. that

D. to

10. She _____ better not arrive late.   A   B   C   D

A. did

B. has

C. had

D. would

11. You _____ forget to pay your taxes.   **A   B   C   D**

A. don't have to

B. have to

C. must

D. must not

12. According to the weather forecast, there   **A   B   C   D**

_____ some rain tomorrow.

A. could

B. may

C. may be

D. maybe

13. A: Do you mind if I borrow a chair?   **A   B   C   D**

B: _____ Do you only need one?

A. I'm sorry.

B. Not at all.

C. Yes, I do.

D. Yes, I would.

14. It's dark out. It _____ be late.   **A   B   C   D**

A. could

B. might

C. must

D. ought to

PART TWO

DIRECTIONS: Each sentence has four underlined words or phrases. The four underlined parts of the sentence are marked A, B, C, and D. Circle the letter of the one underlined word or phrase that is NOT CORRECT.

Example:

Ana <u>rarely</u> <u>is drinking</u> coffee, but <u>this morning</u> she
   A   B   C

<u>is having</u> a cup.
 D

A Ⓑ C D

15. <u>I'd</u> rather <u>having</u> dinner at home <u>than</u> <u>eat</u> out.
    A   B   C D

A B C D

16. My sister <u>may</u> <u>arrives</u> before <u>I can</u> <u>get</u> to the
        A   B   C   D

train station.

A B C D

17. <u>Let's</u> <u>to leave</u> the party <u>early enough</u> <u>to catch</u> the
   A   B   C   D

last bus.

A B C D

18. <u>Could</u> you <u>remember</u> <u>to bring</u> home <u>please</u>
   A   B   C   D

the newspaper?

A B C D

19. You really ought <u>be</u> <u>more</u> <u>careful</u> or you <u>might get</u>
           A   B   C   D

in trouble.

A B C D

20. <u>Would</u> you mind <u>to tell</u> me when you <u>might</u> <u>be</u> late?
   A   B   C D

A B C D

TEST: UNITS 37–38

PART ONE

DIRECTIONS: Circle the letter of the correct answer to complete each sentence.

Example:

Jackie never _____ coffee.   A   Ⓑ   C   D

A. drink

B. drinks

C. is drinking

D. was drinking

1. _____ the mail arrived yet?   A   B   C   D

A. Are

B. Is

C. Has

D. Have

2. She was unhappy because _____ of her   A   B   C   D

friends sent her birthday cards.

A. a few

B. a little

C. few

D. little

3. They didn't have _____ shoes in my size.   **A**   **B**   **C**   **D**

A. a great deal of

B. a lot of

C. much

D. some

4. Can you lend me _____ money?   **A**   **B**   **C**   **D**

A. little

B. some

C. many

D. a few

5. _____ university is larger than a college.   **A**   **B**   **C**   **D**

A. A

B. An

C. The

D. —

6. That's _____ best story I've ever heard.   **A**   **B**   **C**   **D**

A. a

B. an

C. the

D. —

7. _____ music is Jane's favorite pastime.   **A**   **B**   **C**   **D**

A. A

B. An

C. The

D. —

8. You have to protect your skin from

_____ sun.

A. a

B. an

C. the

D. —

A   B   C   D

9. Pauline doesn't eat _____ spaghetti.

A. much

B. many

C. the

D. a few

A   B   C   D

10. **A:** What does David do?

   B: He's _____ accountant.

A. a

B. an

C. the

D. —

A   B   C   D

11. Can you turn on _____ TV? I want to

watch the news.

A. a

B. an

C. the

D. —

A   B   C   D

12. A: I rented _____ video last night.

    B: Oh? Which one?

  A B C D

A. a

B. an

C. the

D. —

PART TWO

DIRECTIONS: Each sentence has four underlined words or phrases. The four underlined parts of the sentence are marked A, B, C, and D. Circle the letter of the <u>one</u> underlined word or phrase that is NOT CORRECT.

Example:

Ana <u>rarely</u> <u>is drinking</u> coffee, but <u>this morning</u> she
    A   B   C

<u>is having</u> a cup.
  D

A   Ⓑ   C   D

13. <u>The</u> news <u>were</u> very sad, and everyone <u>was</u> talking
    A   B   C

    about <u>it</u>.
        D

A B C D

14. Jackie <u>has</u> been <u>a</u> honor student ever since she began
         A   B

    her <u>studies</u> at <u>the university</u>.
        C   D

A B C D

15. I need <u>some advice</u> about what to bring to my
          A

    <u>aunt's</u> house on <u>thanksgiving</u> next <u>Thursday</u>.
     B   C   D

A B C D

16. How <u>many</u> times do I have to tell you not to leave
        A

    <u>your</u> wet <u>shoes</u> on <u>a</u> kitchen floor?
     B   C   D

A B C D

17. Mathematics <u>are</u> Sally's favorite school <u>subject</u>, and
          A   B

    she always <u>gets</u> high <u>grades</u>.
          C   D

A B C D

18. I have <u>a little</u> money, so I can't take <u>a</u> vacation until
       A   B

<u>next</u> year at <u>the</u> earliest.
 C   D

        A   B   C   D

19. We need to pick up <u>some sugar</u> and <u>banana</u> at <u>the</u>
                          A   B   C

supermarket on <u>the</u> way home.
                D

        A   B   C   D

20. Pat turned on <u>the</u> TV in order to see <u>the</u> weather
                A   B

report on <u>an</u> evening <u>news</u>.
         C   D

        A   B   C   D

ANSWER KEY FOR TEST: UNITS 1–4

Note: Correct responses for Part Two questions appear in parentheses ( ).

PART ONE

1. B **2.** C **3.** A **4.** B **5.** C **6.** B **7.** A **8.** D **9.** B

PART TWO

10. D (is taking) **11.** D (wants) **12.** D (like) **13.** B (eats) **14.** B (are you) **15.** A (doesn't)
16. B (she rarely) **17.** D (don't look) **18.** A (always works) **19.** D (feels) **20.** C (is shining)

ANSWER KEY FOR TEST: UNITS 5–8

PART ONE

1. A **2.** D **3.** B **4.** A **5.** B **6.** A **7.** A **8.** A **9.** B **10.** D **11.** C **12.** B **13.** B

PART TWO

14. D (dropped) **15.** A (was) **16.** B (use to) **17.** D (got) **18.** C (got) **19.** A (did you) **20.** B (was driving)

ANSWER KEY FOR TEST: UNITS 9–10

PART ONE

1. C **2.** D **3.** A **4.** D **5.** A **6.** A **7.** A **8.** C **9.** D **10.** B **11.** D **12.** B **13.** C **14.** D

PART TWO

15. A (gets) **16.** D (will tell/is going to tell) **17.** C (I leave) **18.** B (is going to be) **19.** A (won't)
20. D (is going to have/is having)

ANSWER KEY FOR TEST: UNITS 11–16

PART ONE

1. B **2.** B **3.** D **4.** B **5.** D **6.** C **7.** D **8.** C **9.** C **10.** D **11.** B **12.** B **13.** B **14.** D

PART TWO

15. C (worked) **16.** A (has) **17.** A (rented) **18.** D (got) **19.** C (has had) **20.** D (yet)

ANSWER KEY FOR TEST: UNITS 17–20

PART ONE

1. C   **2.** B   **3.** C   **4.** C   **5.** D   **6.** A   **7.** D   **8.** B   **9.** C   **10.** B   **11.** C   **12.** B

PART TWO

13. D (than) **14.** C (perfect) **15.** B (quietly) **16.** B (more interesting) **17.** A (most interesting)
18. C (fastest) **19.** D (unexciting) **20.** A (easier)

ANSWER KEY FOR TEST: UNITS 21–26

PART ONE

1. B   **2.** C   **3.** C   **4.** C   **5.** A   **6.** D   **7.** C   **8.** A   **9.** B

PART TWO

10. C (is) **11.** B (tall enough) **12.** D (to be) **13.** D (to lock) **14.** D (learning) **15.** D (doing) **16.** D (to meet)
17. C (to) **18.** D (remembering) **19.** A (Doing) **20.** C (for)

ANSWER KEY FOR TEST: UNITS 27–36

PART ONE

1. A   **2.** B   **3.** D   **4.** D   **5.** B   **6.** A   **7.** C   **8.** C   **9.** D   **10.** C   **11.** D   **12.** C   **13.** B   **14.** C

PART TWO

15. B (have) **16.** B (arrive) **17.** B (leave) **18.** D (*please* goes after *you, remember,* or *newspaper*)
19. A (to be) **20.** B (telling)

ANSWER KEY FOR TEST: UNITS 37–38

PART ONE

1. C   **2.** C   **3.** B   **4.** B   **5.** A   **6.** C   **7.** D   **8.** C   **9.** A   **10.** B   **11.** C   **12.** A

PART TWO

13. B (was) **14.** B (an) **15.** C (Thanksgiving) **16.** D (the) **17.** A (is) **18.** A (little) **19.** B (bananas)
20. C (the)